G000134823

The Bush Theatre presents the world premiere of

Whipping It Up

by Steve Thompson

8 November – 16 December 2006

Cast

(in alphabetical order)

Alastair	**Robert Bathurst**
Maggie	**Fiona Glascott**
Tim	**Lee Ross**
Guy	**Nicholas Rowe**
Delia	**Helen Schlesinger**
The Chief	**Richard Wilson**
Director	**Terry Johnson**
Designer	**Tim Shortall**
Lighting Designer	**Simon Corder**
Sound Designer	**Fergus O'Hare**
Associate Director	**Tamara Harvey**
Deputy Stage Manager	**Nicole Keighley**
Costume Supervisor	**Caroline Waterman**

Whipping It Up received its world premiere performance at
The Bush Theatre on 8 November 2006.

Robert Bathurst

Robert Bathurst Alastair

Theatre includes *Members Only* (Trafalgar Studios), *Three Sisters* (Playhouse), *Hedda Gabler* (Tour), *Alarms & Excursions* (Gielgud), *Good Copy* (West Yorkshire Playhouse), *The Rover* (Salisbury Playhouse), Channel 4 Sitcom Festival (Riverside Studios), *The Comedy of Errors* (Nottingham Playhouse), *The Nose* (Nottingham and Bucharest), *Noises Off* (Savoy Theatre), *St. Joan, Little Hotel On The Side, Injured Parties, Carrington* (National Theatre), *The Swap* (Boulevard / Soho), *Judgement* (Man In The Moon), *Dry Rot* (Lyric Theatre, West End), *The Next Best Thing* (Nuffield Theatre), *The Choice* (Salisbury Playhouse), *The Importance Of Being Earnest* (Nottingham Playhouse), *Lady Audley's Secret* (Lyric, Hammersmith) and *Getting Married* (Chichester Festival).

Television includes *Cold Feet, My Dad's The Prime Minister, Kingdom, Coup, Poirot, Comic Strip – Sex (Actually), The Stepfather, The Secret, White Teeth, Goodbye Mr Steadman, The Safehouse, Hornblower, Get Well Soon, A Breed Of Heroes, Joking Apart, The Lenny Henry Show, New World, District Nurse, Chelmsford 123, Blind Justice, Red Dwarf, Comic Relief, All In Good Faith, Starting Out, Timeline, Anything More, Would Be Greedy, Lazarus & Dingwell, About Face, No Job For A Lady* and *The House Of Eliot.*

Film includes *Heidi, The Thief Lord, Wind in the Willows, Whoops Apocalypse, Just Ask For Diamond* and *Twenty One.*

Fiona Glascott

Fiona Glascott Maggie

Theatre includes *Hitchcock Blonde, Mahler's Conversation, A Life, The Shaughraun, The Spirit of Annie Ross, The Seagull, Bananas in the Bread Bin, A Midsummer Night's Dream, Three Sisters* and *Romeo & Juliet.*

Film includes *Resident Evil, Veronica Guerin, The Void, Goldfish Memory* (nominated for Best Supporting Actress at the Irish Film and Television Awards*), Judas and Jesus, Fatboy & Twintub* (Special Commendation at the Cork Film Festival), *Forecourt, Meteor, This is My Father* and *Crushproof.*

Television includes *Omagh, Poirot, Jericho, Casualty @ Holby City, Murder in Suburbia, The Long Firm, Fallen, Batchelors Walk, The Bill, Any Time Now, Magnificent Amberson, Fair City* and *Ballykissangel.*

Lee Ross Tim

Theatre includes *Country Music, The Lights, Some Voices, Hammett's Apprentice* (Royal Court), *M.A.D., Christmas* (The Bush Theatre), *The Neighbour* (National Theatre), *Spookhouse* (Hampstead Theatre) and *Bugsy Malone* (Her Majesty's Theatre).

Television includes *Eastenders, The Catherine Tate Show, Jericho, Dunkirk, Hustle, Waking the Dead, Playing the Field, Trial and Retribution, Prods, Shine on Harvey Moon, Thief Takers, SAB, The Negotiator, 99-1, Between the Lines, The Guilty, Shrinks, Work, Shoot the Revolution, Amongst Barbarians* and *Press Gang.*

Film includes *The English Patient*, Mike Leigh's *Secrets and Lies, Goal, Dockers, Dreaming of Joseph Lees, Rogue Trader, Vigo, Metroland, Island on Bird Street, Hard Men, I.D., The Crane, Life's A Gas, Sweet Nothing* and *Buddy's Song.*

Nicholas Rowe Guy

Nicholas trained at Bristol Old Vic Theatre School.

His theatre work includes *See How They Run* (Duchess), *Rosencrantz And Guildenstern Are Dead* (English Touring Theatre), *The Way Of The World* (Wilton's Music Hall), *The John Wayne Principle* (The Pleasance), *The Importance Of Being Earnest* (Nottingham Playhouse), *Twelfth Night* (Sheffield Theatre), *Translations* (Royal Lyceum, Edinburgh), *Black Comedy/ The Real Inspector Hound* (The Donmar @ The Comedy Theatre), *Hamlet* (Hackney Empire and Broadway), *Saint Joan* (Theatre Clywd and West End Gale Edwards), *The Fairy Queen* (Lisbon Coliseum), *Romeo And Juliet* (E.S.C), *My Cousin Rachel* (Derby Playhouse and Cheltenham Everyman).

Nicholas' film credits include *The Baker* (Picture Farm), *Nicholas Nickleby* (United Artists), *Enigma* (Codebreaker Productions), *All Forgotten* (Steve Hills Pictures), *Lock Stock And Two Smoking Barrels* (Ska Films), *True Blue Channel* (Four Films), *Young Sherlock Holmes* (Paramount) and *Another Country* (Goldcrest).

His television work includes *Easy Peasy, Beau Brummel, A Harlot's Progress, Gil Mayo, Waste Of Shame, Our Hidden Lives, Broken News, Princes In The Tower, The Fugitives, The Black Death, Midsomer Murders, La Femme Musketeer, Holby City, Peterloo, Shackleton, Outside The Rules, HG Wells, Longitude, A Dance To The Music Of Time, The Relic Hunters, Let Them Eat Cake, Magpie In The Dock, The Prodigous Hickey, Sharpe's Enemy, Pie In The Sky, Poldark, Dalziel And Pascoe, Kavanagh QC* and *Dangerfield.*

Helen Schlesinger Delia

Theatre includes *The Crucible, The Merchant of Venice, Twelfth Night* (RSC), *Comfort Me With Apples, No Experience Required* (Hampstead Theatre), *Wild East, Bear Hug, The Weather* (Royal Court), *Messiah - Scenes from a Crucifixion* (Old Vic), *Uncle Vanya, A Moon for the Misbegotten, King Lear, The Illusion, Road to Mecca* (Royal Exchange, Manchester), *The Oresteia, War and Peace* (National Theatre), *An Inspector Calls, Inadmissable Evidence* (National Theatre/West End), *The Mill on the Floss* (Shared Experience),

Foreign Lands (Wolsey Theatre, Ipswich), *Beckett* (West End), *The Europeans* (Greenwich/tour), *A Winter's Tale, The Second Mrs Tanqueray* (Salisbury), *Tasso* (Lyric/tour), *Miss Julie* (Plymouth), *Wild Oats* (West Yorkshire), *Design for Living* (Harrogate), *Hamlet* (Compass Theatre) and *Romeo and Juliet* (National and European tour).

Television includes *Trial and Retribution, Doctors, Waking the Dead, Sensitive Skin, The Bill, Dirty War, The Playground, Rose and Maloney, Holby City, The Way We Live Now, Bad Girls, The Greatest Store in the World, Persuasion, Devil's Advocate, Between the Lines, The Cormorant, Harnessing Peacocks, Casualty* and *Bad Girl.*

Film includes *24 Hour Party People.*

Helen won the Best Actress Award in the Manchester Evening News Theatre Awards 2001, and was nominated for Best Actress in the Regional Theatre Awards 2001.

Richard Wilson The Chief

Richard Wilson is best known for his role in *One Foot In The Grave* which has won him numerous awards including a British Comedy Award and two BAFTAs.

Recent television credits include *The True Voice of Prostitution* (More 4/Ch 4), two episodes of *Dr Who* (BBC 1) and the starring role of Dr Donald Neuman in *Born And Bred* (BBC 1). He will soon be seen in *The Acid Test* (BBC) as well as *Kingdom* (ITV).

Richard is a Director, and an Associate Director of the Royal Court where most recently he directed *Rainbow Kiss.* Last year he directed *Primo* at the National Theatre starring Antony Sher which transferred to Hampstead Theatre and then to Broadway. He will direct the film version for HBO/BBC.

In 1994 he was awarded the OBE for services to drama as a director and actor.

Steve Thompson Writer

Steve trained on the RADA playwrights' course. His first play, *Damages*, was commissioned with the support of the Peggy Ramsay Award. It was performed at The Bush Theatre in 2004 and won the Arts Council's Meyer-Whitworth Award for new writing.

In 2005 he was made Pearson writer in residence at The Bush.

He has developed a three part serial for the BBC, a single drama for Granada, a film for Channel 5 and is writing on the new Carnival/ITV serial *Whistleblowers*, due for broadcast in 2007.

Steve is married to the media barrister Lorna Skinner and they live in Hertfordshire with their three children.

Terry Johnson Director

Terry Johnson's work has been performed all over Great Britain and worldwide. He is the recipient of nine major British Theatre awards including the Olivier Award for Best Comedy 1994 and 1999, Playwright of the Year 1995, Critics Circle Best New Play 1995, two Evening Standard Theatre Awards, the Writers Guild Award for Best Play 1995 and 1996, the Meyer-Whitworth Award 1993 and the John Whiting Award 1991.

In recent years he has had eight productions; *One Flew Over The Cuckoos Nest, Hitchcock Blonde, Entertaining Mr Sloane, The Graduate, Dead Funny, Hysteria, Elton John's Glasses* and *The Memory Of Water* running in London's West End. He has twice worked with Steppenwolf Theatre directing John Malkovich in *The Libertine*, which was nominated for five Jeff Awards including Best Production, and *Lost Land*, both plays by Stephen Jeffries.

He has written and directed television drama that has been broadcast worldwide, most recently *Not Only But Always* for Channel Four, which won five International Award nominations, Best Film at Banff, and a Bafta for Rhys Ifans. He wrote and directed *'Cor Blimey*! for ITV. He also wrote *The Bite* for the BBC and ABC Australia. His film *Way Upstream* was chosen for the London Film Festival and *Insignificance* was the official British Entry at Cannes in 1985.

He is Literary Associate at the Royal Court Theatre where he previously directed Joe Penhall's play *Dumb Show* and recently opened his latest play *Piano/Forte*. He is exceedingly proud that his play *Hysteria* is currently featured on a Royal Court 50th Anniversary mug.

Tim Shortall Set and Costume Designer

London work includes *The Overwhelming* (RNT Cottesloe Theatre), *See How They Run* (Duchess Theatre), *The Philanthropist* (Donmar Warehouse), *Telstar* (New Ambassadors*) Elton John's Glasses* (Queen's Theatre), *900 Oneonta* (Old Vic and Ambassadors Theatres), *Body and Soul* (Albery Theatre), *Murder by Misadventure* (Vaudeville and Whitehall Theatres), *Two Boys in a Bed* (Arts Theatre), *A Cook's Tour* (Shaftesbury Theatre), *Twilight of the Golds* (Arts Theatre) and costumes for *The Big Knife* (Albery Theatre), *Excuses* (Soho Theatre), *Disappeared* (Royal Court Upstairs), *Eugene Onegin* (Lyric Hammersmith), *Jeffrey* (Greenwich Theatre), *The Colonel Bird* (The Gate), *What You Get and What You Expect* (Lyric Hammersmith), *Amen Corner* (Tricycle Theatre), and *Singular Women* (King's Head Theatre).

Other work includes *Dead Funny* (Chichester Festival Theatre), *See How They Run* (Theatre Royal Plymouth and tour), Double *Cross* (Michael White Productions), *The Marquise* (Theatre Royal, Windsor and tour), *Martha, Josie and the Chinese Elvis* (Watford Palace), *The Circle* (Oxford Stage Company/Salisbury Playhouse),

The Signalman (Theatre Royal, Windsor), *Amen Corner* (Nottingham Playhouse), *Single Spies* (Theatre Royal, Bath and tour), *Roots* (Oxford Stage Company/Watford Palace – nominated for Best Design, Barclays TMA Awards 1998), *Privates on Parade* (New Vic, Stoke), *Having a Ball* (Birmingham Rep. and tour), *Who's Afraid of Virginia Woolf* (Yvonne Arnaud, Guildford), *The Pit and The Pendulum* (Theatre Royal, Windsor), *Broken Glass* (Watford Palace/Salisbury Playhouse), *King Lear* and *Richard III* (Ludlow Festival), *Goodbye to the Hill* (Liverpool), *How the Other Half Loves* (Watford Palace) and national tours of *The Importance of Being Earnest, The Decorator, Candida, Relatively Speaking* and *Moment of Weakness.*

Designs for dance include new works for The Royal Ballet, Sadler's Wells, Nederlands Dans Theater, Scottish Ballet, Ontario Ballet Theatre, Dutch National Ballet and Norwegian National Ballet.

Television work includes designs for the BBC and NOS Dutch TV – notably winning the RAI Prize for *The Nightingale* (the Netherlands entry in the Prix Italia). Additionally for the BBC, Tim designed *20th Century Blues* – a tribute to Noel Coward – with Robbie Williams, Sting and Elton John.

Simon Corder Lighting Designer

The award-winning lighting designer Simon Corder has had a diverse career: he joined the circus as a ring boy upon leaving school in 1978, later learning his craft as a technician in touring theatre and opera.

Theatre lighting designs includes *Cleo, Camping, Emanuelle & Dick, The London Cuckolds* and *Ends Of The Earth* (National Theatre), *Les Enfants Du Paradis* (Royal Shakespeare Company), *Hitchcock Blonde, Entertaining Mr Sloane, A Streetcar Named Desire* (West End), London productions at the Royal Court, Young Vic, Lyric Hammersmith, Hampstead and The Gate, and for the Theatre Royal Bath and Theatr Clwyd.

Opera includes productions for La Scala Milan, Parma, Ancona, the Ravenna Festival, Cagliari, Buenos Aires, English National Opera, Scottish Opera, Opera North, Welsh National Opera and Holland Park; ten productions for Opera Theatre Company seen in Dublin, London, Paris, Brno, New York, Melbourne. He designed the projections for Operama's *Aida* seen in Europe and South America.

Simon has lit dance productions for The Cholmondeleys and The Featherstonehaughs; for Stephan Koplowitz in London and Essen; for Tanz-Forum Cologne and Yolanda Snaith Theatredance. In 1995 he created an award-winning Night Safari attraction in Singapore Zoo, and in summer 2006 a site-specific event in the grounds of Alnwick Castle, Northumberland.

Fergus O'Hare Sound Designer

Fergus has worked on numerous productions for the National Theatre, Royal Shakespeare Company, Donmar Warehouse, Old Vic, Young Vic, Almeida, Birmingham Rep and West End. Most recent work includes *Rabbit* by Nina Raine (ORL/Trafalgar Studios), Rough Magic's *Improbable Frequency* (Traverse Theatre), *Fool For Love* starring Juliette Lewis (Apollo), *See How They Run* directed by Douglas Hodge (Duchess) and *The New Statesman* with Rik Mayall (National Tour). Forthcoming work includes *King Lear* and *The Seagull* with Ian McKellen, directed by Trevor Nunn (RSC).

Work in New York, Los Angeles and Sydney includes *Hecuba, The Shape of Things, A Day in the Death of Joe Egg, Dance of Death, Noises Off, Electra* (Drama Desk Nominee) and *An Enemy of the People.*

The Bush Theatre

'One of the most experienced prospectors of raw talent in Europe'
The Independent

The Bush Theatre is one of the most celebrated new writing theatres in the world. We have an international reputation for discovering, nurturing and producing the best new theatre writers from the widest range of backgrounds, and for presenting their work to the highest possible standards. We look for exciting new voices that tell contemporary stories with wit, style and passion and we champion work that is both provocative and entertaining.

With around 40,000 people enjoying our productions each year, The Bush has produced hundreds of ground-breaking premieres since its inception 34 years ago. The theatre produces up to eight productions of new plays a year, many of them Bush commissions, and hosts guest productions by leading companies and artists from all over the world.

The Bush is widely acclaimed as the seedbed for the best new playwrights, many of whom have gone on to become established names in the entertainment industry, including Steve Thompson, Jack Thorne, Amelia Bullmore, Dennis Kelly, Chloë Moss, David Eldridge, Stephen Poliakoff, Snoo Wilson, Terry Johnson, Kevin Elyot, Doug Lucie, Dusty Hughes, Sharman Macdonald, Billy Roche, Catherine Johnson, Philip Ridley, Richard Cameron, Jonathan Harvey, Conor McPherson, Joe Penhall, Helen Blakeman, Mark O'Rowe and Charlotte Jones. We also champion the introduction of new talent to the industry, whilst continuing to attract major acting and directing talents, including Richard Wilson, Nadim Sawalha, Bob Hoskins, Alan Rickman, Antony Sher, Stephen Rea, Frances Barber, Lindsay Duncan, Brian Cox, Kate Beckinsale, Patricia Hodge, Simon Callow, Alison Steadman, Jim Broadbent, Tim Roth, Jane Horrocks, Mike Leigh, Mike Figgis, Mike Newell, Victoria Wood and Julie Walters.

The Bush has won over one hundred awards, and developed an enviable reputation for touring its acclaimed productions nationally and internationally. Recent tours and transfers include a national number one tour of *Mammals* (2006), an international tour of *After The End* (2005-6), *adrenalin... heart* representing the UK in the Tokyo International Arts Festival (2004), the West End transfer (2002) and national tour of *The Glee Club* (2004), a European tour of *Stitching* (2003) and Off-Broadway transfers of *Howie the Rookie* and *Resident Alien*. Film adaptations include *Beautiful Thing* and *Disco Pigs*.

The Bush Theatre provides a free script reading service, receiving over 1000 scripts through the post every year, and reading them all. This is one small part of a comprehensive **Writers' Development Programme**, which includes workshops, one-to-one dramaturgy, rehearsed readings, research bursaries, masterclasses, residencies and commissions. We have also launched a pilot scheme for an ambitious new education, training and professional development programme, **bushfutures**, providing opportunities for different sectors of the community and professionals to access the expertise of Bush writers, directors, designers, technicians and actors, and to play an active role in influencing the future development of the theatre and its programme.

The Bush Theatre is extremely proud of its reputation for artistic excellence, its friendly atmosphere, and its undisputed role as a major force in shaping the future of British theatre.

Mike Bradwell   **Fiona Clark**
Artistic Director   Executive Producer

At The Bush Theatre

Artistic Director	**Mike Bradwell**
Executive Producer	**Fiona Clark**
Finance Manager	**Dave Smith**
Literary Manager	**Abigail Gonda**
Marketing Manager	**Nicki Marsh**
Production Manager	**Robert Holmes**
Theatre Administrator	**Nic Wass**
Resident Stage Manager	**Ros Terry**
Literary Assistant	**Raphael Martin**
Administrative Assistant	**Lydia Fraser-Ward**
Box Office Supervisor	**Darren Elliott**
Box Office Assistants	**Gail MacLeod** **Catherine Nix-Collins**
Front of House Duty Managers	**Kellie Batchelor** **Adrian Christopher** **Siobhan King-Spooner** **Glenn Mortimer** **Catherine Nix-Collins** **Lois Tucker**
Duty Technicians	**Jonathan Goldstone** **Tom White** **Sean Wilkinson**
Associate Artists	**Tanya Burns** **Es Devlin** **Richard Jordan** **Paul Miller**
Press Representation	**Alexandra Gammie** 020 7837 8333
Graphic Design	**Stem Design**
Pearson Writer in Residence	**Jack Thorne**

The Bush Theatre
Shepherds Bush Green
London W12 8QD

Box Office: 020 7610 4224
www.bushtheatre.co.uk

The Alternative Theatre Company Ltd. (The Bush Theatre)
is a Registered Charity number: 270080
Co. registration number 1221968

VAT no. 228 3168 73

Be There At The Beginning

The Bush Theatre is a writer's theatre – dedicated to commissioning, developing and producing exclusively new plays. Up to seven writers each year are commissioned and we offer a bespoke programme of workshops and one-to-one dramaturgy to develop their plays. Our international reputation of over thirty years is built on consistently producing the very best work to the very highest standard.

With your help this work can continue to flourish.

The Bush Theatre's Patron Scheme delivers an exciting range of opportunities for individual and corporate giving, offering a closer relationship with the theatre and a wide range of benefits from ticket offers to special events. Above all, it is an ideal way to acknowledge your support for one of the world's greatest new writing theatres.

To join, please pick up an information pack from the foyer, call 020 7602 3703 or email info@bushtheatre.co.uk

We would like to thank our current members and invite you to join them.

Rookie
Anonymous
Neil Adleman
Ross Anderson
Pauline Asper
Lady Constance
    Byam Shaw
Geraldine Caufield
Nigel Clark
Nina Drucker
Ms Sian Hansen
Lucy Heller
Mr G Hopkinson
Joyce Hytner, ACT IV
Robert Israel
    for Gordon & Co.
Hardeep Kalsi
Casarotto Ramsay
    & Associates Ltd
Robin Kermode
Ray Miles
Mr & Mrs Malcolm
    Ogden Radfin
Clare Rich
Mark Roberts
David Robinson
Tracey Scoffield
Councillor
    Minnie Scott Russell
Martin Shenfield
Loveday Waymouth
Alison Winter

Beautiful Thing
Anonymous
Alan Brodie
Kate Brooke
David Brooks
Clive Butler
Matthew Byam Shaw
Jeremy Conway
Clyde Cooper
Anna Donald
Mike Figgis
Vivien Goodwin
Sheila Hancock
David Hare
Bill Keeling
Laurie Marsh
Michael McCoy
John & Jacqui Pearson
Mr & Mrs A Radcliffe
Wendy Rawson
John Reynolds
David Pugh
    & Dafydd Rogers
Barry Serjent
Brian D Smith
Barrie & Roxanne Wilson

Glee Club
Anonymous
Jim Broadbent
Adam Kenwright
Curtis Brown Group Ltd
Richard & Elizabeth
    Philipps
Alan Rickman
John & Tita Shakeshaft

Handful of Stars
Gianni Alen-Buckley

Lone Star
Princess of Darkness

Bronze Corporate Membership
Anonymous
The Peters, Fraser
    & Dunlop Group Ltd
Act Productions Ltd

Silver Corporate Membership
The Agency (London) Ltd

Platinum Corporate Membership
Anonymous

bushfutures
building the theatre of tomorrow...

This autumn The Bush Theatre has launched pilot schemes for its ambitious new training and development programme, bushfutures, providing opportunities for different sectors of the community to access the expertise of Bush writers, directors, designers, technicians and actors, and play an active role in the future development of the theatre.

What to look out for:

The Bush Theatre & National Student Drama Festival
Workshops and masterclasses for student companies at the Edinburgh Festival.

Company Mentoring
Advice and support for an emerging new writing company at the Edinburgh Festival, culminating in a showcase at The Bush Theatre this September.

Bush Activists
A theatre group for 16-18 year-olds, who will study acting, stage management and writing with professional practitioners.

Future Playwrights
Writing courses with Bush writers and staff, culminating in scratch showcase performances.

Futures Directors
An opportunity for new directors to work with professional directors, and participate in **bushfutures** courses.

If you'd like to find out more about how to get involved, please email bushfutures@bushtheatre.co.uk

WHIPPING IT UP

For my children
Isaac, Elijah and Hattie

Characters
in order of appearance

Government:

ALASTAIR, *forty-five, Deputy Chief Whip*
GUY, *thirty-six, Backbench MP*
TIM, *thirty-four, Junior Whip*
MAGGIE, *twenty-seven, researcher*
THE CHIEF, *sixty-five, Chief Whip*

Opposition:

DELIA, *forty-three, Deputy Chief Whip*

Acknowledgements

Thank you to the politicians and journalists who gave up their lunch hours to show me the workings of Westminster: Michael Portillo, Simon Mares, Grant Schapps. Thanks to those inside the Whips' Office who were willing to divulge its secrets but were not willing to be named. Thanks to Matt Flexman and Simon Mitelman for a lunch by the Thames when the idea was born. Particular thanks to Gyles Brandreth, for his generosity and inspiration.

Glossary
Pairing. An arrangement between two MPs on opposite sides of the House not to vote in a particular bill so that their absences cancel each other out. Pairs are often arranged by the Whips' Office.

ACT ONE

Scene One

Music: 'Winter Wonderland' by Peggy Lee.

4 pm. The Upper Whips' Office (Government) inside the Houses of Parliament.

Two doors. One leads to the Member's lobby, the other to the CHIEF's office.

The place has the air of a cramped staffroom in a 1950s public school. A number of old-style wooden desks are placed around the walls and are crammed with junk: cricket pads; crumpled laundry; discarded cups of tea; vote bundles. The walls are oak-panelled; the carpet is worn thin; a meagre light spills through a dirty neo-Gothic arched window. The largest desk in the room belongs to ALASTAIR, the Deputy Chief Whip. There is a sport trophy on it, utilised as a pencil container. On the wall directly behind it is a poster of Luke Skywalker and Darth Vader locked in a light-sabre battle. Someone has made a grudging attempt at Christmas decorations – a prehistoric tree and tatty baubles.

In the far corner is an old black safe with a copy of Who's Who *perched on top. Facing away from the audience is a television that runs pictures from the floor of the chamber – sound turned down. On the wall is a display of tiny photographs of every government MP. The photos are grouped: Prime Minister on the top row; cabinet photos next; everyone else's mugshot in alphabetical order underneath. Black arrows have been scrawled on the diagram to indicate which members of the cabinet have been fired and which backbenchers have been promoted.*

The lobby door opens. Light spills in from the huge, bustling Member's lobby outside. ALASTAIR holds the door open for GUY to enter. ALASTAIR is an immaculate, tanned reptile in a grey flannel suit. He owns the space. GUY *is in pinstripes. He hops in with a fizzy mixture of eagerness and nerves.*

ALASTAIR. I saw your speech.

GUY. You liked it?

ALASTAIR. I saw it all.

GUY. And liked it.

ALASTAIR. Very . . . punchy.

GUY. I was going for punchy.

ALASTAIR. We like punch.

GUY. I thought the joke went pretty well. (*Breath.*)

ALASTAIR. Joke.

GUY. Good reaction.

ALASTAIR. Oh, yes.

GUY. Start with a joke. People told me. (*Breath.*)

ALASTAIR. The opening? That joke?

GUY. Wake the troops up. Get them on side.

ALASTAIR. It was certainly a 'moment'. Did you have people in?

GUY *is confused.*

The gallery. Were there people in? 'Cause sometimes there's a retinue. Mrs Pitcher?

GUY. I'm not married.

ALASTAIR. I meant your mother.

GUY. People don't bring . . . ?

ALASTAIR. You'd be amazed. It's like a teenage talent show. That little thing for Radgely South brings her entire clan when she's down to ask a question. Shops for an outfit first. Puts her hair in rollers. (*Breath.*) Showbiz Mothers, you see. If it hadn't been Parliament it would have been the stage.

GUY. I didn't have anyone.

ALASTAIR (*pointing up at an imaginary gallery*). I thought I saw your . . .

GUY. Friend.

ALASTAIR. Well . . . Lovely. Nice to have a bit.

GUY. Of what?

ALASTAIR. Support. Someone egging you on. First speech in Commons. He looked proud. Your friend.

GUY. What did the Chief say . . . ?

Gestures to the CHIEF*'s door.*

ALASTAIR. Hasn't emerged. But he'll usually pop a note through.

GUY. Fine.

ALASTAIR. Just to say – you know – 'Bravo'.

GUY. Yes.

ALASTAIR. Nice little innings. Got your name up on the scoreboard.

Beat.

GUY. 'Nice little' one.

ALASTAIR. Absolutely.

GUY. 'Nice.' 'Little.'

ALASTAIR. Had them all listening hard.

GUY. Didn't make the boundary, though.

ALASTAIR. Didn't let the side down.

GUY. So: he might have some criticisms.

ALASTAIR. Would that be so surprising? (*Apparently it would.*) You read from notes.

GUY. Oh. And that's a 'thing', is it?

ALASTAIR. Passion is the key, Guy. Passion is what makes the Yeoman of England flock to one's banner on St Crispin's Day.

GUY. I had passion. (*Beat.*) I thought I had passion.

ALASTAIR. But you cribbed it from a filecard.

GUY *doesn't quite see.*

Deeply-felt principles in handy bullet form; lest one forget them. I don't imagine the score at Agincourt would have been quite so favourable if 'Harry', 'England' and 'George' had just been three salient points on an autocue. Now – drinks.

He reaches for a bottle of champagne and pops it open.

GUY. That chap after me spoke without notes.

ALASTAIR. Torwell East.

GUY. And he fumbled.

ALASTAIR. No.

GUY. He didn't?

ALASTAIR. Not at all.

GUY. He got lost and went back. He repeated himself.

ALASTAIR. BBC. When they need the sound bite done again they text you. (*Pouring champagne into silver goblets.*) Pol Roger.

GUY. Yes.

ALASTAIR. Churchill drank nothing else, we're told. Which is a flaming whopper of course; the man used to raid the cleaner's cupboard on a bad night.

Passes the goblet to GUY. *Their hands meet.*

You're suddenly on edge.

GUY. It's the 'drinks'. You're offering.

ALASTAIR. So I am. (*Gently pulls the goblet away.*) And . . . ?

GUY. I imagine I'm about to get my knuckles rapped.

ALASTAIR. Is that what they say?

GUY. Well . . .

ALASTAIR. The tearoom is a crucible of gossip. Three hundred back benchers with nothing to do but wag their Tory chins. I have a sideboard full of champagne and I wanted us to meet. There's no shilling clanking in the bottom.

Finally GUY *accepts his drink.* ALASTAIR *laughs gently.*

'Knuckles rapped.' Be careful with whom you sit. Be careful who's pouring the tea.

GUY (*joining in the laughter*). Yes. There's even a story going round that the Chief kicked a young MP in the voting lobby.

Freeze. ALASTAIR *has stopped laughing.* GUY *follows suit.*

Oh.

ALASTAIR. The man had viral pneumonia. Collapsed on the floor. Before voting.

GUY. And he kicked him?

ALASTAIR. Lord, no! This is the mother of Parliaments.

Breath. GUY *is about to drink.*

Just turned him over with his foot and rolled him through the sheep pen.

A knock on the lobby door and TIM *bursts in. He is an attractive young man in a razor-sharp suit. He has a strong London accent and a streetwise confidence.*

TIM. Deputy?

ALASTAIR (*never once looking round at him*). No, Tim.

TIM. Really?

ALASTAIR. 'Fraid so.

TIM (*points at his watch*). So: approximately?

ALASTAIR. I've only just poured the champagne out.

TIM. I'm just in Member's lobby: sucking off the *Daily Mail*. (*Winks at* GUY.) Nice innings.

GUY. Thanks.

TIM. Should ditch the file card next time.

Exits with the same burst of energy.

ALASTAIR. Timothy Atkinson.

GUY. Mm.

ALASTAIR. Junior Whip.

GUY. I know him.

ALASTAIR. You've met him?

GUY. His father.

ALASTAIR. Of course. There aren't many backbenchers that haven't enjoyed his father's hospitality. Cheers.

Finally they drink their Pol Roger.

Tell me all about Stortford, then. Do you actually live there?

GUY. Lord, no.

ALASTAIR. 'Lord, no.'

GUY. I don't mean . . .

ALASTAIR. Happiness is the sight of one's constituency slowly disappearing in the rearview mirror. (*Relaxes into his chair.*) In mine they manufacture cellophane. Whole place reeks to high heaven of sulphur. I mean, you'd think: country seat; rolling plains. But when you step off the train there's this baleful bloody smell. How 'bout you? (*Breath.*)

GUY. Wholewheat cereal. Constituency smells of breakfast.

ALASTAIR. Milk and honey. Lucky you.

GUY. Yes. Sound people: Stortford.

ALASTAIR. Which only leads me to wonder why you're eager to disappoint them.

Pause.

GUY. Disappoint?

ALASTAIR. When you vote against us. When you vote against the Government tonight.

GUY. Who told you?

ALASTAIR. Well, you did just then . . .

GUY. No, but . . .

ALASTAIR (*tapping his head*). Three hundred and twenty phone numbers – stored here.

GUY. MPs?

ALASTAIR (*shakes his head*). Constituency chairmen. I know all their birthdays. And their wives'. And their Mistresses'. I send a bouquet, an autographed bottle and a cheeky helium-filled balloon. And my remuneration, Guy, is that every time you turn up in Stortford; every time your shirt is un-ironed or your performance is lacklustre my telephone rings.

GUY. My constituency chairman told you I was wavering.

ALASTAIR. Huzzah. (*Breath.*)

GUY. It's a matter of conscience actually . . .

ALASTAIR. Just wait whilst I dig out my dictionary, will you?

GUY. The bill . . .

ALASTAIR. . . . has had two readings and an interminably detailed committee stage. You come at me with 'Conscience', and I find myself wondering why you've only just acquired one. Mince pie?

He offers one. GUY *declines.*

Haven't we taken care of you? That swanky office in Portcullis House . . .

GUY. A swivel chair and an Anglepoise lamp isn't going to buy my vote tonight.

ALASTAIR. I wasn't aware it needed buying. I thought your blue rosette was some sort of tiny clue to your allegiance. (*Half laugh.*) It's basically 'tent poles', isn't it? Whether the people of England can put up their tent poles. (*Beat. He fixes* GUY *with a strong stare and smiles.*) This is it. I'm doing it. Whipping. This is all that it actually entails. Drinks; warm smiles; a plate of mince pies. A shepherd and one lost sheep. Really all quite civilised.

Pause. He is waiting for GUY *to speak.*

GUY. It's this prohibitive tax . . . Semi-permanent dwellings.

ALASTAIR (*amused*). Gazebos, trailers, tents and awnings. Mm?

GUY. We plan to tax them.

ALASTAIR. If they stay up for more than eight weeks at a time.

GUY. Fifty-seven days; seems rather arbitrary.

ALASTAIR. The Minister had been staring at a sauce bottle.

GUY. Look . . .

ALASTAIR (*with emphasis*). Travellers, Guy. They're evolving. We're not just talking a trailer and a washing line. They're organised. They're buying land. They're marking out roads. The farmer next door is bound to be a Tory. Taxing a man for his awning and guy ropes is bound to exert a measure of control.

GUY. My local scouts will have to fork out thousands – they have a brick-built loo and a row of permanent wigwams.

ALASTAIR. And you think – I'm sorry to ask this – but you think that's enough to compel you to defy us? (*Breath.*) It's what the Chief calls a 'nuts and bolts' bill. Government ticking over. Not exactly legislative history.

GUY. Did you see the protesters?

ALASTAIR (*shakes his head*). No, I came in through the Sally Gate. Scared you, did they? Dear, dear. With their chunky socks and windcheaters.

GUY. I got pelted.

ALASTAIR. Eggs?

GUY. Marshmallows. They're toasting them out there on the pavement.

Beat.

ALASTAIR. So: you're voting against us to stop members of the Camping Lobby pelting you with confectionary.

GUY. I have concerns that . . .

ALASTAIR. Can we get on to the real reason? The reason we lost your vote tonight.

GUY. I've just told you.

Beat. They both know he is lying.

ALASTAIR (*soft, like a disappointed nanny*). Lying in this room, Guy, is never anything short of utterly disastrous. (*Leans in.*) Shall we call it a beginner's blunder? A reflex lie, blurted out. Like children often do. 'Who put muddy footprints on the sofa?' 'Not me, Daddy.' What you expect from children?

GUY. What makes you think I'm lying to you?

ALASTAIR. You have a television. Same as I do.

Beat. GUY plays dumb.

Lunchtime news. A trigger-happy farmer. Two teenagers walking on his winter crops. Bang bang. And suddenly the bill is poison. Suddenly you're looking for a reason to desert. (*Pause.*) Well?

GUY (*coming clean*). A girl with a gunshot wound will be all over the papers.

ALASTAIR. Now we're getting somewhere.

GUY. I . . .

ALASTAIR. You're worried about how it looks, Guy. You're worried how it looks for *you*. (*Beat.*) We have a lot like you: well-meaning; ultra-charming; plenty to offer. Only one things holds them back – the desperate desire to do what's popular.

TIM *bursts through the door again.*

TIM. Deputy.

ALASTAIR. Spiffing.

TIM. There's a hoo-ha on the floor.

ALASTAIR. Well, thank God you came to me 'cause as you know I'm Mr Hoo-Ha . . .

TIM. Someone's drawn a penis on the dispatch box.

ALASTAIR. And it's sparked some sort of constitutional crisis?

TIM. Front bench women are refusing to speak there . . .

ALASTAIR (*under his breath*). Then we should have drawn penises long ago, shouldn't we?

TIM. I offered to prop a book against it, but . . .

ALASTAIR. Find the Chief. Get him to sort it.

TIM. Can't.

ALASTAIR. Why?

BOTH. He's getting changed for Santa.

Beat. Finally ALASTAIR *turns.*

ALASTAIR. Why's *he* Santa, for God's sake?

TIM. Barnado's. That fat bloke off the telly blew us out.

ALASTAIR. Biggins?

TIM. Flu.

ALASTAIR. And we can't get anybody else?

TIM. Like?

ALASTAIR. Famous, fat and Tory. (*Breath.*)

TIM. Russell Grant?

ALASTAIR *stares at him.*

Two out of three.

ALASTAIR (*to* GUY). Excuse me.

ALASTAIR *swans out.* TIM *finishes off* ALASTAIR'*s champagne. He walks over to the* TV *monitor and turns it up. A debate can be heard from the floor of the house.*

MAN. '. . . progress has been made on private bank debt and bilateral debt through the European agencies, and this has been very significant and helpful. However, we should bear in mind the words of Sir Edmund Holgate-Stuckey . . . '

TIM (*bored with it*). Jesus.

> TIM *turns the sound down. He plonks himself in his place with his feet on the desk. His desk is a bombsite – empty drink cans and magazines. He eats his way through a box of cheese straws left over from a Christmas party. A long pause.* GUY *looks away. Every time he looks up again* TIM *is grinning at him.*

> You're Stortford, aren't you?

GUY. Yes.

TIM. Seventy thousand. Forty-three per cent. Bell weather. Always swings with Number Ten. What is it: glue you make there?

GUY. Wholewheat cereal.

> *Beat.*

TIM. Down in my place it's a brewery. Whole town stinks like an old pub table. Can't stand beer, me. Don't expect you ever eat breakfast, do you? (*Eats, reads a newspaper and whistles the tune of 'Winter Wonderland'.*) We're used to these last minute stunts. Little pirouettes. 'Daddy's not watching.' Always have to jump about like prats and scrape up one or two stray votes. We're not worried. (*Beat.*) You don't seem like the sort to waver, though.

GUY. You mean principled.

TIM. Or demented. Yeah.

GUY. I happen to think the bill is cruel and arbitrary.

TIM (*not looking up*). And you happened to switch on the telly at lunchtime. (*Amused, never aggressive.*) You burn down a Three-Line Whip in your first six months in office, you total plum – it's not respect you're gonna get, it's a permanent place in obscurity. Just so as you know. (*Eats.*) Don't be fooled by the nicey-niceness. The champagne and the patter. 'Are you a chap or not?' Once the door is shut, we're not gentleman politicians any longer.

GUY. I don't think I'm the only one to hop the fence.

TIM. We've got plenty of contempt to go round, believe me.

GUY. Only takes a little mistletoe to strangle an oak tree.

TIM. And we can fuck up your career with three phone calls. Got any other poncey metaphors?

Beat. GUY *visibly takes offence and gets up to leave.*

Nibbles.

Pause. GUY *turns and stares.*

The Deputy does 'drinks'. I do 'nibbles'.

GUY. Nibbles?

TIM. I invite people in. I make nibbles. Interested?

GUY. In what?

TIM. A nibble.

He offers GUY *a cheese straw. Pause.*

GUY. Pardon?

TIM. The fast track. The route to the top. Junior Minister by thirty-seven. Cabinet by thirty-nine.

GUY. Nibbles?

TIM. I carry a list. A small list. A list of reliable folk. The nibbles people. (*Beat.*) Men who are willing to go over the top and into battle. You walk through the lobby on a leash tonight and I put your name down for nibbles.

GUY. You can't be serious.

TIM (*tilting back in his chair*). What happens on the floor of Commons every time a Minister falls flat on his arse; drowns at the dispatch box; fumbles; fights for his words – someone always pops up and rescues him. Some backbencher makes a dick of himself, right? – toadying; grovelling; ask-a-silly-question; raising a lunatic point of order so the Minister can regroup and get his breath back.

GUY. Nibbles.

TIM. That's them.

GUY. It's a code.

TIM. Woah. Lightning fast.

GUY. For people who bail you out on the floor.

TIM. 'Come down and have some nibbles.' It means 'Come down and get your assignment.'

GUY. And there's a reward?

TIM. Largest donator to the Tory Party read me all my bedtime stories. A parent like mine carries some very serious clout around here, believe me.

Beat.

GUY. So you can get me . . . ?

TIM (*drawing three imaginary steps in the air, starting at the top*). Party – constituency – conscience. The only thing that trumps all three is personal gain. (*Breath.*) 'Conscience' isn't a factor, really. Just means an MP's wife has been nagging him. (*Pause.*)

GUY. Junior Minister.

TIM. They come to us for recommendations.

GUY *offers his hand to shake.* TIM *won't take it.*

A handshake is a sign that a man isn't armed. An MP is honourable.

GUY (*withdrawing his hand*). Nibbles, then.

TIM. See you in the lobby.

Beat. GUY *nods and slowly exits.* TIM *reclines in his chair and sings like a football fan – clapping above his head.*

(*Singing.*)
'Sleigh bells ring, are you listening?
In the land snow is glistening.
A beautiful sight – we're happy tonight,
Walking in the winter wonderland.'

Yes!

ALASTAIR *enters.*

ALASTAIR. There's a Beaver Patrol out there cooking sausages and hurling them at Cromwell's head.

TIM. I saw.

ALASTAIR. They're singing 'Little Drummer Boy'. Round a gas stove.

TIM (*amused*). Gazebos, trailers, tents and awnings.

ALASTAIR'*s Blackberry buzzes in his pocket and he answers it –* TIM'*s does the same simultaneously.*

ALASTAIR. What's the time?

TIM. Four. When's voting?

ALASTAIR. Maybe nine. Debate at seven-thirty. Seven amendments to vote.

TIM. We reached a final total for today, then?

ALASTAIR. Five.

TIM. Five!

ALASTAIR. I know. Hardly Watt Tyler, is it? Five rebels.

TIM. Shame he couldn't have shot 'em both. If the other pikey hadn't run for help no one would know . . . They'd both have bled to death in a cabbage and we'd be safe home.

ALASTAIR. She's a cruel mistress – Dame Lunchtime News.

TIM. Got to say it's bloody bad luck. Pissy little bill like this.

ALASTAIR. God is not a Tory.

TIM. Go on then – reel them off for me.

ALASTAIR (*off the top of his head, numbering on his fingers*). Lewis.

TIM. Just for a change!

ALASTAIR. Penhale, Brookes.

TIM (*points at the lobby door as number four*). Blokey there.

ALASTAIR. And . . .

BOTH (*almost in unison*). Allendorf.

Beat.

TIM. Emphysema might rule him out from voting.

ALASTAIR. By nine tonight? I admire your optimism.

TIM. His breathing's getting pretty erratic.

ALASTAIR. Well unless it stops completely before teatime we'd better have words. (*Looks at the photo board and points at the faces.*) Lewis, Penhale, Brookes.

TIM. Blokey.

ALASTAIR. And Allendorf.

TIM. Usual unstables, then.

ALASTAIR. Take the temperature. Steady the nerves. Phone their families. Surround them with the faithful. Most of them just want a bit of lovin'.

TIM. You're a rock, Deputy.

ALASTAIR. Come through it too many times. Majority of three. They push us to the precipice every single time. Tom Brookes can be bought back easily – you settle all his bar bills within a square mile of here. He'll be nine parts pissed when he votes. Most times he doesn't even know what he's voting for.

TIM (*half laugh*). Yeah . . .

ALASTAIR. Joyce Penhale. Bovine Joyce. Turned down for two ministerial appointments, entirely on the grounds of her uncanny resemblance to a Friesian. They're insecure. All of them. Treat them as you would a child with a tantrum. (*Indicates the lobby door.*) What happened here then, whilst I was gone?

TIM *is smiling.*

What?

TIM. Four minutes.

ALASTAIR. You bagged him?

TIM. Four minutes fifteen seconds. Yo!

ALASTAIR. Don't keep score, Tim. I absolutely hate it when you keep score.

TIM. Four minutes fifteen and back in the fold.

ALASTAIR. What d'you do for him?

TIM (*shrugs*). A sort of greatest hits package. 'Daddy's not watching.'

ALASTAIR. That's one of mine.

TIM. Well . . . I add a little twist in the mix, there. Hope you don't mind.

ALASTAIR. I'd like to think I set it up.

TIM. If it makes you feel better by all means, but I slam-dunked it.

   ALASTAIR *stops what he's doing and looks over. The atmosphere grows colder.*

ALASTAIR. Whipping's not a contact sport, Tim.

TIM. No.

ALASTAIR. Many things we need to teach you – top of the list would be taming that swagger. (*Looks at his watch.*) Brookes next, I think. (*Trying to command* TIM's *attention.*) Maybe you can track down Lewis whilst I'm with him. What else?

TIM. I've still got my woman loitering.

ALASTAIR. Woman?

TIM. My 'woman'.

ALASTAIR. Loitering.

TIM. Out in the lobby.

   Beat.

ALASTAIR. I can't start taking tea with every researcher brought to orgasm by one of our boys.

TIM. I can get her to describe the details. Anything juicy – anything unusual.

ALASTAIR. And then what?

Pause. TIM *glances at the safe.*

Tim.

TIM. All right . . .

ALASTAIR. Dear Tim . . .

TIM. Yes, OK.

ALASTAIR. The rapier not the sword.

TIM. So you keep saying.

ALASTAIR. We don't stride up to Her Majesty's representatives with a bludgeon in one hand and a list of their faux pas in the other.

TIM. They all know about the safe though, don't they?

ALASTAIR. And the fact that they know is sufficient, don't you think?

TIM. We're gonna need everyone on side.

ALASTAIR. The threat of the threat. We don't open it for every tiny crisis. I'm going to go and see Penhale after Brookes.

TIM. You?

ALASTAIR. Chief can do Allendorf – the PM can sweep up the stragglers.

TIM. When he makes it back.

ALASTAIR. I beg your pardon?

TIM. When the PM returns from his trip.

ALASTAIR. Which is likely to be . . . ?

TIM. There was a delay.

ALASTAIR. Don't tell me.

TIM. The President's golf cart ran over his toe. Put things back a bit. Quick X-ray; bandage . . . you know.

ALASTAIR. So: he's going to miss the vote.

TIM. Well, maybe.

ALASTAIR (*under his breath*). Man's a bloody liability.

TIM. The Leader of the Opposition is honour bound to pair if he's late back.

ALASTAIR. And that makes it rosy?

TIM. No, but . . .

ALASTAIR. I don't care about his vote, Tim. I object to taking our side out to bat without him. OK, let's use the opportunity. Careful how you sell it. Say 'Undisclosed location'. PM's with the President at an undisclosed location. Then they might think we're off to war . . . Iran or somewhere.

ALASTAIR exits. TIM clears away the goblets and the champagne. He accidentally leaves his Blackberry on the desk and exits whistling the 'Gloria' from 'Ding dong merrily on high'. After a pause there is a knock at the lobby door. Beat. Another knock. MAGGIE enters. She is a petite young woman in a formal skirt and blouse with a commons ID card that says 'Government Researcher'. Her skirt is rather too short for it to be accidental. She carries a folder and a tiny bundle of tissue paper.

Her eyes dart around to observe every tiny detail of the room. She strokes the safe as if it were a holy relic. She sees the wall of photos and her attention is caught by one of them – a cabinet member. The black arrow beside him indicates he has recently been demoted. She takes a pin off the board and sticks it in his face. Beat. TIM's Blackberry buzzes on the desk. MAGGIE stares at it.

TIM *rushes in.*

TIM, Oh. I thought . . .

MAGGIE *has a curiously girlie voice.*

MAGGIE. I wasn't sure if I should come straight in, or . . .

TIM. I thought we said the terrace.

MAGGIE. I'm sorry.

TIM. No. Never mind. Here now. (*Breath. He collects his Blackberry.*) How 'bout drinks? Champagne? Mince pie or something?

She unwraps her tissue paper bundle. Inside is a small ceramic hippo. She places it on her palm. TIM *turns round with her drink and sees it.*

What the hell is that you've got there?

MAGGIE. Say 'hello' to Mr Hippo.

Scene Two

Music: 'Happy Holidays' by Andy Williams.

5 pm. The Upper Whips' Office. The TV monitor is on, sound turned down.

The CHIEF *is sitting at* ALASTAIR*'s desk, nodding gently with a tumbler of whisky in his hand. He wears a Santa suit without the wig and beard. He is an imposing man with a sour, ruddy complexion. Sweat has made his hair soggy.*

ALASTAIR *enters from the Member's lobby in his coat and carrying his umbrella. It has been raining. He sees the* CHIEF *and deliberately slams the door at a medium volume to wake him.* ALASTAIR *radiates calm.*

ALASTAIR. How'd it go?

CHIEF. I'd rather eat my own liver than wear that acrylic wig again. Where in God's name was Christopher Biggins? Can't imagine he's run off his feet.

ALASTAIR (*hangs up his coat*). Was it torture?

CHIEF. I don't mind a few naughty toddlers. Making kids cry reminds me I haven't lost my edge. It was the bigger girls. Thirteen-year-olds. Low-slung jeans.

ALASTAIR. Mm-hmm.

CHIEF. Bellybuttons out. If they're gonna dress like sirens . . .
I'm not a pervert, Alastair, but I am still a man. Had to stop
the kids from sitting in my lap after an hour in the grotto.

ALASTAIR. Mm . . . That was probably wise.

Beat. The CHIEF *drinks.*

CHIEF. Did you know that Barbie has her own horse and
carriage now? 'Mazing. I used to get a penny and an
orange.

ALASTAIR. Why d'you do it?

CHIEF. Chairman's wife. Daft tart. If I see Biggins I plan to
kill him. With pain. (*Drinks.*) Lord, Christmas is a trial.
(*Points at* ALASTAIR*'s TV screen.*) Phoned twice to get my
monitor fixed. Staff too pissed to answer.

ALASTAIR. Welcome to watch mine.

CHIEF. What's been happening then; whilst I've been
dispensing Barbie's new accessories? Everyone's calm
which usually mean we're flagging. In fact, the calmer the
Whips the deeper the crisis and you're bloody radiant.

ALASTAIR. How are you, Chief?

CHIEF. How do you mean, specifically?

ALASTAIR. How are you feeling?

CHIEF. Rather patronised.

ALASTAIR. I meant your health.

CHIEF. Alastair, can we be men about this? Can we shelve my
health issues, just for one day?

ALASTAIR. Chief . . .

CHIEF. It's an occupational hazard: too many late nights;
too many fat cigars. Heart attacks are de rigueur. If I was
a carpenter I'd have splinters. Change the song.

ALASTAIR. Chief . . .

CHIEF. If you really want to talk about health, answer me this . . . Did you have the beetroot soup last night?

ALASTAIR. I had the blinis.

CHIEF. Christ! State of my toilet. Thought I was haemorrhaging. Santa had red stools.

ALASTAIR. Chief . . .

CHIEF. And that steak did me no favours. I've seen animals with less life get up off the road and walk away.

ALASTAIR. Chief . . .

CHIEF. You tell me why our boys are on manoeuvres. Stop trying to cosset me – I'm already done up in cotton wool.

Beat.

ALASTAIR. There's been a change.

CHIEF (*antennae suddenly pulsing*). Go on.

ALASTAIR. Five.

CHIEF. Abstaining?

ALASTAIR. Against us.

CHIEF. On the 'Ging Gang Goolie' bill?

ALASTAIR. Five Tories up in arms this afternoon.

CHIEF. About the rights of Gyppos? I thought this was going to be a steal.

He slams down his drink.

ALASTAIR. We're on the march. All right? I don't want you developing a thing.

CHIEF. You don't want me developing a thing?

ALASTAIR. I mean . . .

CHIEF. . . . dropping down dead before my vote's in. Don't treat me like an invalid, Alastair. Reel them off for me. (*Numbering on his fingers.*) Brookes and Lewis . . .

ALASTAIR. Obviously. Penhale, Allendorf . . .

CHIEF. I thought Allendorf was dead.

ALASTAIR. If wishing made it so. (*Continuing.*) Pitcher.

CHIEF *looks quizzical.*

He's new.

CHIEF. Little worm.

ALASTAIR. It's sorted. We've got four back. Enough for a majority. (*Breath.*)

CHIEF. What made them run for cover?

ALASTAIR. You didn't see the news?

CHIEF. My grotto had no media access – strangely.

ALASTAIR. Wiltshire farmer. Taking pot shots at a pair of kids.

CHIEF. Oh Jesus.

ALASTAIR. Two travellers.

CHIEF. Damned lucky that it only stopped at five.

Beat.

ALASTAIR. We've paid Brookesy's bar bills.

CHIEF. Again. And Lewis? School fees up, are they?

ALASTAIR. I said we'd reach into our pockets.

CHIEF. What about Joyce Penhale?

ALASTAIR. Straight sets.

CHIEF. The poor bag is just drooling for that first promotion. She's got one of those husbands that keeps cornering me. Tells me he sees a whole different side of her. I wanted to say that that was bleeding obvious, since he shares a bed with her and we think she looks like a dairy cow. What d'you give her?

ALASTAIR. Select Committee. Farming.

CHIEF. Huh.

ALASTAIR. She didn't catch the irony.

CHIEF. And Allendorf?

ALASTAIR. Well . . . Thereby hangs a tale . . .

CHIEF. Dodgy ticker. Emphysema. Piles.

ALASTAIR. God is laughing at us now.

CHIEF. Think we might have to kill him off ourselves. My
God, it's all changed. It's not like we're enforcers any more
– majority of three after that selfish tit from Fairstone
dropped down dead in his Gaspacho. Everyone knows we're
fumbling. On the eve of a shitty bill like this and they turn
up with their shopping lists. (*Breath.*) Want me to dine
Allendorf, do you?

ALASTAIR. You know him of old, Chief.

CHIEF. You mean I handled his balls at prep school. How did
you get the new chap. Pitcher, was it?

ALASTAIR. Tim bagged him.

CHIEF. Shit. He'll be showing off all night, then.

ALASTAIR. Oh, I think Tim is basically sound. He needs . . .
grooming.

CHIEF. Needs a crash course in how not to get on my tits.

ALASTAIR. He's been chalking up some very big successes.

CHIEF. And how is he achieving those, I wonder.

They exchange a glance.

I picked his name out of the hat, you know.

ALASTAIR. Tim?

CHIEF. That Christmas present thing you do.

ALASTAIR. Secret Santa.

CHIEF. Would you believe it? I get bloody Timothy. Thought
maybe I'd buy him a course of elocution. (*Goes to refill his
glass.*) He made a balls up with the pairing. Did you see?
The witch from Norwich went ballistic.

ALASTAIR. It was my fault.

CHIEF (*quietly and deliberately*). We both know that's
    bollocks. Is she coming here: your opposite number?

ALASTAIR (*checking his watch*). Any minute.

CHIEF. On her broom. Don't you dare shoulder the blame for
    him!

ALASTAIR. Chief . . .

CHIEF. I know you, Alastair. You've sat and watched *Spartacus*
    far too many times. Let the Juniors pay for their gaffs.

ALASTAIR (*unconvinced*). Well . . .

CHIEF. If she's flying in then I best get moving, sharpish. (*He
    picks up the telephone. Beat. He has forgotten the task that*
    ALASTAIR *has set him.*) Tell me again, will you?

ALASTAIR. Allendorf.

    CHIEF *dials.*

CHIEF (*on the telephone*). Roger Allendorf. (*Beat.*) The Chief
    Whip. (*Hand over phone. To* ALASTAIR.) Still makes them
    hop. (*Breath.*) Hello Roger! It's Fulton. Free for dinner?
    (*Beat.*) Members' room. Say six. That's splendid. Yes. Yes.
    (*Pause.*) Well, I didn't expect so. (*Beat.*) Of course I was
    disappointed. No doubt you have your reasons. (*Pause.*)
    Really? Well, of course we take it seriously. (*Pause.*) Well . . .
    that's very eloquent. Poetic, even. Yes. (*Beat.*) Yes. Six,
    then. Chateau Briand's back on.

    Puts the phone down. ALASTAIR *is scowling.*

    I'll go without pudding.

ALASTAIR. I'm not your wife.

CHIEF. Stop acting the part. I saw you frown. I had an apple
    and a peach for lunch.

ALASTAIR. Super.

CHIEF (*points at the phone*). Arsehole knew why I was
    phoning. Quotes bloody Kipling at me. 'Mistletoe can kill
    an oak.'

ALASTAIR. That what he said?

CHIEF. Mm.

ALASTAIR. 'Mistletoe'?

CHIEF. Can you believe it? 'Mistletoe can kill an oak tree.

ALASTAIR. Never knew it was Kipling.

CHIEF. You've heard it.

ALASTAIR. Joyce Penhale said it to me.

The room freezes over.

CHIEF. Those exact words.

ALASTAIR. About half an hour ago.

CHIEF. Moo face?

ALASTAIR. I did the usual 'disappointment'.

CHIEF. And she said . . .

ALASTAIR. 'Mistletoe can kill an oak tree. We had better be sure to take her seriously.'

Pause.

CHIEF. You don't think . . . ?

ALASTAIR. Yes.

CHIEF. You think?

ALASTAIR. Yes.

CHIEF. Really?

ALASTAIR. Don't *you*? Unless there's been a sudden run on Rudyard Kipling. Two rebel MPs reading from the same script. Ought to give us at least a moment's pause. (*Beat.*) They move in herds out there – won't take much to convince me that these five rebels sat in a room. Not if they're reciting the same bon mots. Now, what we need to focus on . . .

CHIEF. Is who was paying for their dinner?

They walk to the photo board and study it. ALASTAIR *runs his forefinger across the photos, focusing on Cabinet Ministers. The* CHIEF *looks over his shoulder at the faces.*

ALASTAIR. Tiny majority. And a bill about as popular as galloping dysentery. Who decided to seize the moment? Launch a concerted attack?

ALASTAIR*'s finger pauses on the face into which* MAGGIE *has stuck a pin. He pulls it out and regards the face. He turns and stares at the* CHIEF.

You don't think . . . ?

CHIEF. Titwank.

A knock at the lobby door. The two men instinctively start to whisper.

ALASTAIR. Knickers.

CHIEF. It's not her?

ALASTAIR. Yes.

CHIEF. The Norwich witch?

ALASTAIR. Indeed.

CHIEF. Well I'm not staying to apologise just for being male. (*He darts for his office door. In a loud whisper.*) We need to get one of the rebels in. Sweat him. That new bloke. You think he might blab if we . . . ?

ALASTAIR. What!?

CHIEF. It's ten past five. Civility's a luxury, Alastair. Time to polish off all our rubber truncheons. If five have already declared then there could be ten or fifteen more by the division.

ALASTAIR. I'll text the boys. Take a head count.

CHIEF. We knew this day was coming.

ALASTAIR. You think . . . ?

CHIEF. No one gives a fart about Travellers. It's a fucking leadership challenge. Plain and simple. Someone's trying to make us stumble. (*More knocking.*) Get Pitcher back here. We'll strap him to a chair. Do that routine of yours.

ALASTAIR. 'Prisoner next door.'

CHIEF. 'Prisoner next door.' Have I got time to change out of Santa?

ALASTAIR. I don't think 'jolly' is where we want to be aiming.

ALASTAIR *starts to write a message on his Blackberry. Another knock at the door.*

(*Shouting at the door.*) One moment. (*Whispered to the* CHIEF.) I'm going to need to push the vote late. So the PM's back from Florida.

CHIEF. He's not still . . . ?

ALASTAIR. Don't go there.

CHIEF. When d'we want it?

ALASTAIR. Say ten. Ten-thirty maybe. Three-hour debate. Ten minute speeches. (*Looks at his watch.*) So . . . I need upwards of twenty speakers. Then the PM will have time to race over from the airport.

CHIEF. Get her to agree to a dozen. Twelve speakers each – give him time to floss and take a dump first.

ALASTAIR *tugs the lobby door open –* DELIA *is there; an attractive English rose in her early forties. She is dynamic and smart in a navy suit. Her voice is like cold steel.*

DELIA. Was it so late, friend, ere you went to bed that you do lie so late?

CHIEF. Why's she calling you 'friend'?

DELIA. Oh, you peasant.

She strides in.

CHIEF. You're looking very elegant, Delia.

DELIA. Fuck off, will you?

CHIEF. Fair enough, I suppose.

He exits into his office. ALASTAIR *is staring at* DELIA *in mock horror at her swearing.*

DELIA. You know what happened. You've heard about the gaff.

ALASTAIR. It was my gaff.

DELIA. Oh don't even bother.

ALASTAIR. Twelve years since we needed a Pairing Whip. You had such a big majority you could practically vote on a rota.

DELIA. Tim offered me a pair.

ALASTAIR. I'm aware. Yes.

DELIA. I had an MP with a family wedding to attend. And Timothy offered me a pair.

ALASTAIR. Please don't feel that you have to repeat the whole story.

DELIA. Exactly the same pair he offered the Lib Dems. *And* the Scottish Nationalists. And we all accepted. Tim wiped out three MPs with just one of yours.

ALASTAIR (*quietly*). Very creative . . .

DELIA. I beg your pardon?

ALASTAIR. Deeply shocking!

DELIA. Don't dare smirk at me.

ALASTAIR. I wasn't smirking. That was shock.

DELIA. That was pretend-shock covering a smirk!

ALASTAIR. Tim is very keen to impress.

DELIA. I'll leave my shoes by the door and he can shine them for the morning. All pairing's off, as of now. When the cricket season starts you can forget it. I shan't be releasing anyone.

ALASTAIR *clutches his heart in mock sorrow.* DELIA *gets out a letter and shows it to him.*

I've written to the Leader of the House, of course . . .

ALASTAIR. I wish you hadn't done that . . .

DELIA (*talking over him*). . . . demanding a formal apology.

ALASTAIR (*perusing the letter*). Well, this is inaccurate,
Delia. Tim's not to blame at all.

DELIA. Whose name should I put here, then?

ALASTAIR. Mine.

DELIA (*with contempt*). *You're* Spartacus?

Beat. DELIA *shakes her head and folds the letter away.*
ALASTAIR *gestures her to a seat.* DELIA *clears a space
amongst the detritus.*

Do love what you've done with the place. Five years I
worked here. Fresh flowers. Matching pencil tin and in tray.
Six months in office and you've turned it back into a public
school dorm. Where do you boys keep the pornography?

ALASTAIR. I realise opposition isn't quite the same frenetic
whirlpool as government, but if your sole purpose for the
afternoon is coming here and making trouble would you
mind if we rescheduled?

Beat. They begin work.

DELIA. Seven-thirty start. Seven amendments to vote tonight.
How many speakers?

ALASTAIR. Twelve.

DELIA. The week before Christmas?

ALASTAIR. Wives in town; everyone wants to step up when
their partner's in the gallery.

DELIA. Everyone? I heard tell of rebels . . .

ALASTAIR. Don't start . . .

DELIA. You should phone round.

ALASTAIR. It's not nice to smirk. I do agree.

DELIA. Serve you right for this footling legislation. Where
does Santa come off running a Three-line Whip on it?

Trying to win the diehards back, are we? Seasonal bout of kicking the minorities?

ALASTAIR. Now look . . .

DELIA. Tory faithful are worried, aren't they? Too much modernising by the PM too soon. You want to remind them all that you still know how to deal with loafers and shirkers.

ALASTAIR. Delia . . .

DELIA. She was just fourteen.

ALASTAIR. I didn't put the gun in his hand.

DELIA. Damned sure you put the thought in his head, though.

Beat.

ALASTAIR. Interesting to note you've so much time on your hands you can spend it minding my business . . .

DELIA. I'm prepared to stretch to twelve. To match your twelve. Twenty-four.

ALASTAIR. And we start at seven-thirty?

DELIA. And a vote at maybe . . . ten?

ALASTAIR. Ten is good for me, actually. (*Breath.*) Maybe . . .

DELIA. Yes?

ALASTAIR. Ten-thirty.

DELIA. That works.

Pause. They are both suspicious.

ALASTAIR. Up to you.

DELIA. No you.

ALASTAIR. No you.

DELIA. No you.

ALASTAIR. No.

DELIA. You say.

ALASTAIR. No you say.

DELIA. You.

ALASTAIR. I'm happy to let you . . .

DELIA. As am I.

Silent suspicion.

ALASTAIR. Maybe . . . shall we say . . . eleven?

DELIA. Sure. Eleven. Great.

ALASTAIR. Great.

DELIA. Great.

ALASTAIR. Eleven.

DELIA. Eleven it is.

ALASTAIR. Fine.

DELIA. Fine.

Pause.

BOTH (*perfect unison*). Twelve?

DELIA (*explodes*). What the hell is this about, Alastair? Why d'you need to run so late tonight?

ALASTAIR. Same question!

DELIA. Got some stragglers who can't make it over?

ALASTAIR. I can smell your duplicity when you come in the door.

DELIA. You've got one in a monastery, haven't you? A dypso, drying out. Is he coming back on a donkey?

ALASTAIR. Last time you pulled this stunt you had one in bed. We were waiting on his orgasm.

DELIA's mobile rings. ALASTAIR points to it.

Him again?

She exits to the lobby to take her call. ALASTAIR hurriedly fetches a book secreted in a locked drawer. He thumbs through it – it's a desk diary. He smiles and taps the page he has been looking for. He goes to the lobby door and opens it – DELIA is standing in the doorway with the phone pressed to her ear, thumbing through an identical book.

Unions dinner.

DELIA (*hanging up*). Just wait a second . . .

ALASTAIR. December twenty-first, it says here. You've got seventy Labour MPs being dined tonight in Paddington. They want to stay for coffee and mince pies.

DELIA. I've hired two coaches. They could be back in an instant.

ALASTAIR. Eight minutes from the time that the bell goes. You can't scam me, Delia – I've got all your guys' wedding anniversaries logged here.

DELIA. Well, what's your excuse then?

ALASTAIR *opens his mouth to speak.*

Don't help me. More than eight minutes in a cab. No one's birthday. No one's hernia . . . (*She is glued to her diary. She flicks back a couple of pages, pulls out a Post-it note and waves it victoriously.*) Where's the PM then?

ALASTAIR. On hand . . .

DELIA. You've got a rebellion to quash and your leader's on an aeroplane. (*She steps up to him – intimate, almost sexual.*) There's only one person in the world who's as skilled at this as you – it's just a bugger that she's your opponent.

A silent standoff.

ALASTAIR. We'll say eleven then. Your guys can have their mince pies.

DELIA. And your boss can enjoy his in-flight movie.

ALASTAIR. Anything else or are we done? (*Under his breath.*) Want to rip my heart and lungs out whilst you're here?

DELIA (*under her breath*). Ooh please. If you're offering . . .
(*She goes to exit and stops by the door.*) Happy Christmas,
then – in case I don't see you.

ALASTAIR. Thank you.

DELIA. You in Dorset?

ALASTAIR. No, actually – I'll be here. Someone has to man
the fort. The London flat. Waitrose turkey loaf for one.
(*Breath.*) You?

DELIA. Marks and Spencer.

TIM *enters suddenly. He stops short when he sees her.*

Too much aftershave, Tim. Whips and waiters shouldn't
wear it. Distracts from what you're selling.

She exits.

TIM. Was she peed off?

ALASTAIR. She was lovely about it.

TIM. The pairing thing, I mean . . .

ALASTAIR. Tim! – Don't worry about it. It's fine.

TIM *is still unsure.*

TIM. Guy Pitcher's outside. Did you need him?

ALASTAIR *runs over to the* CHIEF's *office door, knocks
once and opens it.*

ALASTAIR (*shouting offstage at the* CHIEF). Get cracking.
(*To* TIM.) Send him in, then.

TIM. What's happening?

ALASTAIR. 'Prisoner next door.'

TIM *exits. A moment later* GUY *enters.*

Welcome.

GUY. You wanted to see me again.

A loud bang from the CHIEF's *office. Like someone
slamming a book on a desk.*

ALASTAIR. I'm grateful.

GUY. Tim explained . . .

ALASTAIR. We'd got your vote back. We've been celebrating.

He ushers GUY *to a chair.*

CHIEF (*offstage, furiously angry*). Christ!

GUY *falters for a moment before sitting down.*

ALASTAIR. Chief is rather preoccupied. One or two stragglers still to sweep up.

CHIEF (*offstage*). You bloody pansy!

ALASTAIR. But I wanted to express my formal gratitude.

Bang. Loud thump against the desk next door.

And also: some information.

CHIEF (*offstage*). You anaemic debilitated weasel! You dare look me in the eye and say that?

ALASTAIR. Something . . .

CHIEF (*offstage*). Where's your bloody loyalty?

ALASTAIR. . . . you might be . . .

CHIEF (*offstage*). You're dead meat!

ALASTAIR. The Chief would like a short word when he's finished.

Enormous bang.

GUY. Finished what exactly?

CHIEF (*offstage, a long drawn-out cry*). Suffer!

ALASTAIR (*charming – a wide smile*). Talking to the other rebels.

Scene Three

Music: 'Let It Snow' by Dean Martin.

7 pm.

ALASTAIR *is interviewing* MAGGIE. *She sits with the small ceramic hippo perched on her knee and a folder tucked under her arm.* TIM *is loitering.* ALASTAIR *seems rather bored.*

MAGGIE. 'I dream of your thighs.'

ALASTAIR. That's five.

MAGGIE. Yes.

ALASTAIR. Five syllables. Haiku is seventeen. I don't wish to appear ungrateful but if you have the rest of the poem . . .

MAGGIE. That's just the first line.

Beat.

ALASTAIR. 'I dream of your thighs.'

MAGGIE. 'Maggie, golden starlight girl.'

TIM. Her name is mentioned.

MAGGIE. Yes.

TIM. In writing.

ALASTAIR. Really?

TIM. She has it in writing. With his signature.

ALASTAIR. Does it get any better than 'thighs'?

MAGGIE. There's twenty-five poems.

TIM. All on postcards.

MAGGIE. Left lying in my in tray. Presents sometimes.

TIM. Show the Deputy Mr Hippo.

She holds it up.

MAGGIE. I found it on the dashboard of my car.

TIM. Paints a fascinating picture, yeah?

ALASTAIR. The haiku and the hippo.

TIM. I'll say. Not regular behaviour. For a Minister. Stalking one's researcher.

MAGGIE (*self-effacing*). I do mostly photocopying.

TIM. Sure.

> ALASTAIR *strolls over to the photo board and looks at the photo – the man in whom she stuck the pin. Beat. Turns.*

ALASTAIR. Is it Margaret?

TIM. Maggie.

ALASTAIR. Girl can answer for herself, Tim. What is it your friends call you? Meg?

MAGGIE. Well, no. They tend to use my name.

ALASTAIR. 'Maggie'?

MAGGIE. Mm.

ALASTAIR. Really?

MAGGIE. Mm.

ALASTAIR. 'Maggie.'

TIM. Shall I do drinks?

ALASTAIR. We tend to have an aversion to it. The name, I mean. 'Maggie.'

MAGGIE. Oh. Really?

ALASTAIR. You understand why, of course. Shadow looms large. Certain names drop from the canon. (*Breath.*) Can I call you Peggy?

MAGGIE. No.

ALASTAIR. Peg? Mags?

MAGGIE. Can I ask you something? What do you plan to do with this? (*Breath.*) My haiku. My ceramic hippo.

TIM. It's got a message on his bum.

ALASTAIR. Let me ask *you* something.

MAGGIE. Sure.

ALASTAIR. Why?

MAGGIE. 'Why?'

ALASTAIR. Why?

MAGGIE. 'Why' what exactly? (*Breath.*) Why am I here? I'm a loyal Conservative.

ALASTAIR. The Party.

MAGGIE. I hear murmurs: he's started making trouble for you. Ever since the PM chucked him out of the cabinet job.

ALASTAIR (*making light of her concerns*). Three hundred and twenty Tories. Very few have actual job titles. Everyone's plotting their rise.

MAGGIE. Tim said that there's a full-scale rebellion.

ALASTAIR (*eyeing* TIM). Gosh, how very informative.

TIM. She just wants to lend a hand.

ALASTAIR. And you assumed that the best way to do it was to bring me your personalised hippo.

MAGGIE. Don't you have some sort of safe here . . . ?

She regrets her sudden eagerness. Pause. ALASTAIR *is totally unresponsive.*

You don't seem all that interested.

ALASTAIR. Have you any idea how many times I've had this little chat? 'He broke my heart.' 'Went back to his family.' 'Left me with nothing, now I'm hoping the Whips can help me shaft him.'

TIM. Look . . .

MAGGIE. We didn't have an affair.

ALASTAIR. It's just that you're just a loyal Conservative.

MAGGIE. Believe me . . .

ALASTAIR. No one ever waltzes through that door without bringing in their own specific agenda. (*Beat.*) I'm sorry. It's terribly nice of you. But would you take your seventeen syllables out of here.

TIM. Surely today is an exception?

ALASTAIR. Tim . . .

TIM. With this stuff we could pressurise . . .

ALASTAIR (*to* TIM). Speak not another word! (*To* MAGGIE.) We're not street-traders shelling out for gossip. I'm sorry you've been misinformed.

MAGGIE (*staring straight at* TIM). What were you going to say? (*Beat.*) 'Today is an exception. We could pressure . . . '

ALASTAIR. I've just told him to be silent.

MAGGIE's voice changes – she suddenly becomes harder and colder.

MAGGIE. Does he do other stuff? Beg and roll over?

An icy pause. TIM *is lost for a moment.*

TIM. I think, maybe . . .

ALASTAIR (*to* TIM). You are a gargantuan tosser. (*To* MAGGIE.) What is it this time, dear? *Sunday Mirror*? *Newsnight*? Tabloids? TV? Hippo was a nice touch. Really. Did you stay up all night and write those? (*To* TIM.) It's the Holy Grail for Fleet Street. Get the Whips to shed light on their methods. At the last count the BBC were offering a five-figure bounty.

Beat. MAGGIE *laughs quietly.* TIM *is aghast.*

MAGGIE. *Observer.*

ALASTAIR. Oh. How splendid. An exclusive. On the office.

MAGGIE. Yes.

ALASTAIR. And you came to see us at play.

Turns to TIM *with a disappointed expression.*

TIM. Deputy . . .

ALASTAIR (*raises his hand to silence him*). Dear Tim . . . Go and compose a haiku. One that employs the words 'gullible' and 'tosser'.

MAGGIE (*counts on her fingers*). 'S your first line, right there.

Beat. TIM *exits.*

ALASTAIR. Reveals his hand rather too fast. Makes him vulnerable to pretty girls like you. So, then. You thought you'd worm your way in here with your short skirt, your thin blouse and your name that we find warmly appealing.

MAGGIE. How d'you know?

ALASTAIR. He said you were eager to meet me.

MAGGIE. Too eager?

ALASTAIR *shrugs.*

'K. I'll be more laid back next time.

ALASTAIR. And wear a false nose and a wig. I might remember you from this debacle.

He gets up and goes to the lobby door to show her out. She doesn't budge. Instead gets out a notebook.

MAGGIE. September the twelfth. MP for Coneelly was petitioned for divorce.

ALASTAIR. Was he now?

MAGGIE. He'd been wavering on voting with the government. You paid his legal bills. He's supported you ever since. Yes?

No response.

OK. July three. Barely a month into the new government. A national daily tabloid ran an entrapment scheme, sending a reporter to MPs with cash for questions. Reporter met with three Tories. All three fell for it. The paper didn't print it though. The Editor-in-Chief, however, is rumoured to be named in the New Year's Honours list. (*Beat.*) Can you confirm these stories?

ALASTAIR. Have you managed any photocopying at all whilst you've been here?

MAGGIE. I have nine separate incidents logged. Whips buying votes. Saving face. Nine in four months.

ALASTAIR. And you are hoping I'll be your source.

MAGGIE. Paper won't print unless a high-ranking Whip . . .

ALASTAIR. How very restrained.

MAGGIE. Unless someone confirms. You won't be named.

ALASTAIR. I realise. Because I won't be confirming.

Beat.

MAGGIE. You have a fund. Yes? (*Breath.*) Bankrupts can't sit in Commons. You bail out MPs. Credit cards. Bar bills.

ALASTAIR (*indicates door*). Would you mind?

MAGGIE. Even sent some drunkard to dry out in a monastery?

Silence. Nothing from ALASTAIR.

More than one desk in this office. Your chips are spread ever so thin.

ALASTAIR. Apparently.

MAGGIE. All I need . . .

ALASTAIR. Is a front page and a byline. I'm sorry I that I can't jump-start your career.

MAGGIE. The poems are real.

ALASTAIR. Lucky you – a foot in our door. Must have been doing the lambada when Tim rang.

MAGGIE. He's quite smitten.

ALASTAIR. Well . . . your baby voice and hemline are very persuasive tools, so bravo you.

MAGGIE. A leadership challenge. By stealth. By the back door. I can deliver the challenger.

ALASTAIR. He is no one now. He's just a hairdo and a prayer card. A handful of names he's mustered. We've spent the last three hours corralling them. He may feel rather foolish when he's looking round tonight for friends. The rebellion is crushed.

Points at the Star Wars *poster.*

MAGGIE. Don't those guys there win?

ALASTAIR. In the film. In reality Skywalker's career took a nosedive.

This time he makes sure – he takes her bag from her and walks over to the door with it. She stands.

MAGGIE. Everything they say is true, then? Black ties; cigar smoke; whisky in cutglass. Westminster runs the country. But the Whips run Westminster. The cabinet is the veneer.

ALASTAIR. Three hundred and twenty egos. Without us, party politics would just curl up and die. You want to make us grotesques – you waltz in here with titbits, hoping I'll rub my hands. What you forget – you folk – is that no business ever runs without HR.

MAGGIE. Come on . . .

ALASTAIR. Sometimes we bully – sure – but most of the time it's just about sitting down and listening. Who else but a Whip is going to know an MP's strengths and foibles; who else is going to take the time? These people are career politicians – oftentimes they need a guiding hand on the rudder. There's nothing dishonourable.

MAGGIE. And yet you keep your work a secret. Doesn't quite add up to me. Every Whip sworn to keep Mum – if it's so above board then how come you treat it like espionage?

She nods at the safe.

ALASTAIR. Say nothing, my dear, and you give the impression of knowing everything.

He hands back her file.

MAGGIE. There's more to it. Majority of three. The Whips hold all the power – you can make or break the law. Three quiet conversations in this room are all it takes to turn the tables. Democracy's in that champagne.

ALASTAIR. You tell me, what would you rather? Another twelve years sitting under a landslide. A healthy opposition . . .

MAGGIE. . . . just means we surrender our government to you and your bag of tricks.

ALASTAIR. Time to pop back to *The Observer* and return their blank cheque.

MAGGIE (*a final plea*). One nod. One little word.

ALASTAIR. Hard to believe, I know – nothing, not even a threat to our party makes a whip betray his code.

The CHIEF *bursts in from his office. He is wearing a grey pinstriped suit.*

CHIEF. Alastair.

ALASTAIR (*to* MAGGIE). Would you excuse me?

MAGGIE. I'll wait outside.

ALASTAIR. I think we're done anyway. Thank you so much for stopping by.

Beat. MAGGIE *exits.*

Distractions we don't need. You look . . .

CHIEF. Don't I? Just had my wearisome dinner with Allendorf. How that man is still living I don't know. Takes him half an hour to lift his steak knife off the table.

ALASTAIR. You get him back?

CHIEF. Every illness known to science, but still has the energy to bite us in the arse at the division bell. (*Beat.*) Anyway . . . looks like we're afloat again. The other four . . . all definites?

ALASTAIR. Everyone back in their prams.

CHIEF. Last thing we need before Christmas is a bill going 'cunt up'. Goose on Christmas Day – don't want it spoiled! (*Beat.*) I appreciate it, Alastair.

ALASTAIR. Sorry?

CHIEF. Brookes, Penhale, Lewis. I appreciate your work. I should have been . . .

ALASTAIR. You were dishing out Barbie dolls, weren't you?

CHIEF. You know what I'm saying: I've not had my head in the game.

ALASTAIR. We stand or fall as a unit.

CHIEF. I'm trying to say the 'T-word'.

ALASTAIR. Let's imagine that you've said it then, shall we? (*Reaches for a bottle of champagne.*) All we need to focus on now is how much champagne we have to order for the party later.

TIM *walks in through the lobby door just as* ALASTAIR *is pouring. He is oddly quiet and dazed.*

Tim-lad!

TIM. It's more than five.

A nasty pause.

ALASTAIR. What?

TIM. I was checking my card – doing rounds. I knocked on Molyneux's door.

ALASTAIR (*suddenly bristling with energy*). It's more than five? (*Breath. He wants* TIM *to respond.*) You're saying Molyneux as well, are you . . . ?

TIM. I had to read upside down. A memo on his desk. From Mills.

ALASTAIR. Mills too?

He grabs a pen and a Post-it note and starts to scribble the names down.

TIM. Memo on his desk – I couldn't make it out. Long list of names. Something about a second wave.

CHIEF. What?

TIM. I was only in there for second but I'm telling you – we should be bracing ourselves for more. (*Beat.*) If you wanted to rock the Government you wouldn't come down the mountain on a steed – you'd dress it up in all the usual petty bargains . . .

ALASTAIR. Tim . . .

TIM. Keep us looking one way – leave our main flank unprotected.

ALASTAIR (*pencil poised*). Who?

TIM. They chose them deliberately, those five – the usual gang of malcontents: the ambitious; the dispossessed.

ALASTAIR (*pressing him for the list of names*). Tim, quickly!

TIM. All the time we've been piddling around and there's an army outflanking us.

CHIEF. What the hell . . . ?

ALASTAIR (*to the* CHIEF). He's saying we've been scammed. (*To* TIM.) I need names.

TIM. You'll need a bigger piece of paper too.

A knock at the door. MAGGIE *enters.*

MAGGIE. Excuse me. Did I leave my . . . ? (*She spots her hippo on* ALASTAIR's *desk.*) Ah, yes.

She retrieves it and leaves.

TIM. Think we should offer her a drink now?

ACT TWO

Scene One

Music: 'Mary's Boy Child' by Harry Belafonte.

9 pm. The UPPER WHIPS' *Office. The sky is dark. Christmas tree lights have been turned on. The only other illumination comes from the TV monitor.*

The CHIEF *and* TIM *sit and watch the debate in the flickering light. The sound is turned down. The* CHIEF *has a fixed expression – a mixture of calm and contempt: his 'Debate face'. He has a tumbler of whisky in one hand and he swirls the liquid round in the glass from time to time. There is a cricket stump lying across his lap.*

TIM *has stripped down to his shirtsleeves. His lips twitch occasionally as if mouthing the inaudible words that the speakers on the floor are saying. Long pause whilst they watch in silence.*

TIM (*bothered by what he sees, a long low sound*). Ooh. (*Another long pause.*) Ooh.

> *The* CHIEF *turns and eyes* TIM *suspiciously.*

> (*Sharp intake of breath.*) Ffff . . .

CHIEF. Would you mind buggering off, Timothy?

TIM. Sorry. (*Pause.*) Ah . . .

CHIEF. Look, go and sit in the bar if you want to regale the world with farmyard impressions.

TIM. Right-ho. (*Pause.*) Ooh.

CHIEF. Are you looking to get slapped?

TIM. I'll be quiet.

CHIEF. If you want to keep both of your kneecaps, yes you will.

Breath. TIM *gets up and attempts to turn up the sound. The* CHIEF *growls quietly.* TIM *leaves it and sits down again.*

TIM. He's doing OK. I mean, I can't actually hear it but . . .

CHIEF. He hasn't fallen over. That's the measure of oratory now, is it? Content's neither here nor there this evening, Tim. Tonight's about the timing.

TIM. Icelandic airspace, last I heard.

The CHIEF *stares at him.*

It was the President's golf cart. Broken toe. Purple nail. Not serious. He'll be limping when he makes it back, that's all. Leading us to victory in one shiny shoe and one slipper. (*Beat.*) Not your ideal choice for PM. I mean I understand why, of course. Who doesn't? He's very . . . next door. (*Breath.*) Labour benches all stuffed full of accountants and salesman. Our side is a Jacobean play. Should have someone Gothic to play the lead.

CHIEF. Maybe if we nudge him off the terrace and into the Thames.

TIM. No . . .

CHIEF. Three hundred and nineteen of us. You can get a man topped for a grand in the Mile End Road.

TIM. I meant . . .

CHIEF. Three quid each. Would hardly break the bank, would it? Shall I pop a note round after prayers?

TIM (*light, not malevolent*). It's not been going too smoothly. A little light business and we can't even push it through. I'm just exploring the idea that the guy may sometimes be . . .

CHIEF. More of a hindrance than a help?

TIM. We must have known this day would come! He's not 'proper' – he's just got an easy style. All that crap with the bike! We put him up front as a veneer. Plenty of old gargoyles in Cabinet biding their time – hoping he would win the election, then expose himself as lightweight so that they could step in and take the reigns. Only surprising thing is, it's taken six months for one to show his head above the parapet.

CHIEF. And what do you think our role should be? Would you care to enlighten me at all? You think we're Kingmakers. Just pop into the Royal bedchamber – brandishing daggers – when we decide he's outlived his time. We're supposed to be the rock, you titbrain. Last men left standing when he's taking hits from all sides. We are nothing when our loyalty is gone.

TIM. I was just commenting.

CHIEF. Yes, I know what you were commenting. Turd. You think if we take the night off and go out on the piss there'll be a new and better PM by morning.

TIM. Now, Chief . . .

CHIEF. What bloody use would we be? What power would we have as enforcers round here, if we press-ganged these numpties into voting and they thought they could slip us a tenner to look the other way? All we have is our unswerving devotion – they think we're fanatics who will come for them in their beds. Don't you start throwing your support behind this other tit. Not 'til he's on the throne. Aim for his balls. (*Drink to his lips.*) You're extraordinary. No doubt about it. Half-worm and half-weasel. There's a sideshow somewhere with an empty stage.

TIM (*inaudible*). Oops.

CHIEF. It's the price of holding the keys. Sometimes – many times – we see the party on its knees. We see it 'cause we're trusted to see. Kind of implicit with that trust that we're not gonna start a fucking coup. (*Mumbles.*) You're only here 'cause your father knows how to find his chequebook in a hurry. Wasn't my idea to ask you.

They watch in silence.

TIM (*pointing at the screen*). East Polson.

CHIEF. Mm.

TIM. Tinned soup?

CHIEF. And sauces. Yes.

TIM. Fifty-nine percent. Eight successive wins.

CHIEF. You've already pissed me off. Don't waste your breath trying to impress me.

TIM slumps back in his chair. Pause.

TIM. Deputy looks calm.

CHIEF. Doesn't he ever?

TIM. Presumably he does have a game plan.

He looks at the CHIEF, *hoping for enlightenment. No response.*

What about the safe?

CHIEF. The safe?

TIM. Someone's birthday. Isn't that the code?

CHIEF. Kind of desperate, aren't you? To root through everyone's linen.

TIM. What other tricks are up our sleeve?

CHIEF. Two types in this office, Tim-lad: the ones on their way to somewhere else and the ones who are staying. I knew which you were, soon as you arrived. It means you're not always in the loop.

TIM. I love this job as much as anyone.

CHIEF. No. *I* love this job, Tim. To you it's a stepping stone. No politics in this room: don't make speeches; don't legislate; don't have views. We exist solely to enforce. Massive political ambition – zero political content. Keeps us pure. (*Breath.*) Shrewd move – your dad getting you in here. One place you're never going betray yourself as dumb.

TIM. You don't know me . . .

CHIEF. You know why I work here? I'm passionate about Conservative ideals. Etched somewhere in marble pillars is the truth about this country: we're a nation of achievers. Left wing want us all sitting hugging each other – dragging our sick and wounded alongside. But you can't chain nature down – we're not pack animals, we're people and the strongest should be left to roam free. I believe it – not because some focus group told me to – it's what I believe! And I'll spend my career making it real. You're not here because you love this job at all – you're an angry little weakling with a grudge and an overbearing dad.

TIM *is beaten into an angry silence.*

Sent you to posh schools, didn't he?

TIM *looks up sharply.*

I've read the file. What did they do? Flush your head down the lavatory? Call you names 'cause you ate off your knife. Eh?

TIM. 'Sweep.' They called me 'Sweep'.

CHIEF. As in the dog.

TIM. As in the chimney.

The CHIEF *laughs cruelly.*

CHIEF. Bunch of horse-faced toffee-nosed boys have given you a grudge that's roughly the size of Panama. Daddy buys his way into our circle and you get a safe seat for your birthday – wrapped in a bow. (*Breath.*) I'm here because I'm a believer, Tim. You just want to get your own back on the world.

TIM. Right. Well, thanks for the lecture. Look forward to toasting you at your retirement do.

CHIEF. You don't scare me, you little shit. Your father could be Lord God Almighty but I'm Chief Whip! The Pope couldn't get a bloody table in the Member's bloody dining room. And I've got one permanently reserved. Do your stint, earn your stripes, and then get the hell out of my office, will you?

TIM. I've had a higher strike rate since I've been here than any of the seniors.

CHIEF. And how have you achieved that, I wonder? Got some little scam going, have you? Baubles from Dad. Handing

out promotions here and there – how many Ministries have
you assigned already? – A big stick or a sugar lump. How
long can you sustain it?

TIM. What's the alternative?

CHIEF. The alternative is Whipping! Stare them straight in the
eyes and demand that the bastards comply! You want to
treat it like some sort of sales pitch – voting for your party's
not like choosing a sodding fridge-freezer. There is no
choice! It's like drawing breath. All I have is my certainty –
and it's a damned persuasive tool. (*Relaxes. Grumbling
quietly.*) You have no faith; no creed; no certainty. This will
never be more than a line on your CV . . .

TIM *is suddenly distracted by something that appears on
the screen. He jumps up.*

TIM. Eh?

CHIEF. Indeed.

TIM. No but. What?

CHIEF. Yes, thank you Tim.

TIM. They didn't call it.

CHIEF. No. Right.

TIM. They didn't call the vote on that amendment. Seven
amendments to vote before the big one. Buy us some time.

CHIEF. Uh-huh.

TIM. I thought that was the whole point, wasn't it?

CHIEF. Are you under the impression I rose to this rank by
knowing sod all about procedures?

TIM. I thought . . .

CHIEF. I know. I know they didn't call it. I was watching.
Same as you were. Somehow I managed not to wet my
pants. (*Gestures to screen.*) Focus on Alastair. Learn from
him, as long as you're with us. Learn some self-control.

He pats the chair beside him. TIM *reluctantly sits.*

He's a good chap to have on the floor. Look at the way he conducts the business. The angle of his feet. The casual observer would never clock that the suave reclining gentleman on the right side is actually running things. Lifts his toe to tell them to round off now; rotates the anklebone if he wants them to carry on a while. It's a fine art. I've never mastered it at all. I just used to grab 'em by the vest and pull. Nothing more insanely unpredictable than an MP with a camera in his face. Have to have a Whip in with them; like a colt without a jockey otherwise. Runaway stagecoach. You just watch and learn.

Long pause.

TIM. I chose him.

CHIEF. Chose. Who?

TIM. The Deputy. Secret Santa. Drew his name. Can't think of what to buy. He never seems to want for much. I thought a posh dinner, theatre tickets, but you never see him with . . . you know: 'someone'. (*Beat. No response.*) Seemed rude: buying dinner for one.

CHIEF. He lives and breathes this office – and he's perfect for it: affable in spades. He doesn't want his private life all cluttered up – not when he's got you to nursemaid every day! (*Drinks.*) The Whips are like wife and family. Only place in Commons with a sense of group identity. You do this job with hatred, Tim. For Alastair it's pure love. His faith is the strongest of all.

TIM *springs up suddenly and glances at his watch.*

TIM. Bleedin' hell! It just happened again there!

CHIEF. Calm down . . .

TIM. Half an hour we've lost by not voting that time. The poor sod will be in baggage reclaim when it comes to . . .

CHIEF (*picking up the cricket stump and pointing the sharp end*). Sit your arse down. I'll hurt you if I have to. (*Beat.*) I'm serious, Tim. Many a Junior Whip found himself on the business end of a genuine George Yates.

TIM. We're not calling any amendments? I thought we were trying to spin things out for a while.

CHIEF. And then umpteen new rebels declare.

TIM. So now we're speeding things along? (*It dawns.*) Ah . . .

CHIEF. You haven't heard?

TIM. The Union's Christmas Beano.

CHIEF. We're collapsing the debate, young Timothy. Pulling the rug. There are seventy Labour votes stuck up in Paddington. Napkins tucked in collars, merrily gorging on bread sauce and chipolatas; fully expecting us to spin out our seven amendments until eleven o'clock. But by the time they move on to plum pud we'll be taking a lap of honour. It's what they call a dirty trick. Not 'sophis', but effective all the same. Learn to keep your mouth shut. We might just let you in from time to time.

Beat.

TIM (*starting to smile*). We lied.

CHIEF. See, now you're happy. Now you're back in the know.

TIM. I thought we only lied in an emergency.

CHIEF. What sort of crises have you lived through that they've been any bloody worse than this? Majority of three, you penis. Majority of three. Six months into the session. Some ex-Minister wants to be King of the Castle. I will use my every aching sinew – my heart, lungs, liver, ten fingers and ten toes, including the gouty one – to make damned sure that all our business is tied up in a neat little parcel by the time I hit my pillow. And if that means I am forced to renege on some word of mouth agreement that Alastair made at teatime then so be it. Delia can suck a fart out of my bumhole! She's not a real witch anyway, we just pretend she is. Could have her in a fight. (*Beat.*) You're smirking.

TIM. I like being on the clever side.

CHIEF. Winning isn't hard. You've just got to punch lower than the other bloke.

Knock at the lobby door. Beat. TIM *strides over to open it.*
GUY *rushes in. He is completely out of breath.*

TIM. You OK? What's wrong?

GUY *can't speak.* TIM *is amused.*

This is that scene from that film.

CHIEF. What?

TIM. Dustin Hoffman. Opens his door.

CHIEF. Get the bloke some champagne.

GUY (*gasping for breath*). No . . .

TIM. Really?

CHIEF. Celebrate!

GUY. Can't.

TIM. Really?

GUY. Dozens of them.

TIM. No. That other film. About the Zulus. Oh, what was it called now?

CHIEF. That film about Zulus? Take a wild guess.

TIM. 'Dozens of Zulus.' 'Hundreds of the blighters.' Can't do Welsh.

GUY. Toilet.

TIM. What?

GUY. Been in the loo.

CHIEF. Oh well, that's certainly big news.

TIM. And? What's in there that's so special?

GUY. Dozens of Zulus.

TIM. In the loo?

CHIEF (*laughs. Pause. His face falls*). How many? How many Zulus? (*He comprehends.*) Seventy.

TIM. Oh, my Christ.

CHIEF. They're hiding in the fucking toilet. (*Beat.*) Can you think of another film, Tim? Where our heroes get taken up the arsehole.

The lobby door flies open. DELIA *is there looking smug.*

DELIA. Boys.

CHIEF. You're a cheating bloody tart and I despise you.

DELIA. Say what's on your mind, Fulton. Don't just fanny around with words.

CHIEF. You've been hiding your men in the bogs tonight.

TIM (*pointing at the screen*). Jesus. Look. Here they come.

DELIA. I know. It's unconscionable.

CHIEF. Shitter.

The men stare open-mouthed at the monitor.

DELIA. To think I'd have the poverty of spirit to suspect you boys of a dirty tricks campaign! To think I'd even suggest you were capable of pulling the debate whilst I wasn't looking. It's not playing by the rules. Just be happy you were blameless.

TIM. Have you come in here to crow?

DELIA. My lads had to forego their turkey but I told them it would be worth it. 'Tent poles' being crucial.

CHIEF. You have to win everything! How petty!

DELIA. Oh, hello Mr Pot! Have you been introduced to Mrs Kettle? You're the one who stuck a Three-Line Whip on it. Only reason you're pissy now is 'cause I scammed you. (*Looks at the screen.*) Yikes! Even Alastair's struggling. To look confident, I mean. Any second now . . .

A ringing sounds in the room: halfway between a buzzer and a bell. It gives one short three-second burst.

Ah, there we go. The old emergency bell rings. The familiar sound of 'What in the name of God do I do?'

The bell rings again.

CHIEF. Arse . . .

DELIA. They've been sitting in my office since teatime. We've had a scrabble tournament and shove h'appeny. Proper rules, from the MP from Tween. And of course we've jollied ourselves along by imagining your reaction. Quite a wild afternoon, really. Been too long since I had a game of sardines.

CHIEF. Well, I'm truly appalled . . .

DELIA. That I beat you? I dare say you are. The pain may lessen in time.

CHIEF. I'm appalled by the tactics.

DELIA. Don't push it. I've had six months of you bastards; calling a vote on my birthday; calling a vote when my period's due. Not a single dirty wheeze escapes you, Fulton. So don't you do that righteous load of old balls. It's not the dirty trick that bothers you; it's getting shafted by a girl.

CHIEF. And you a student of Westminster College.

DELIA (*getting right in the* CHIEF'*s face*). You think I don't know? Arsehole. Think I don't know who planted the 'Witch' rumour?

TIM *sniggers. She turns on him.*

Who made the little pointy hat from newspaper and stuffed it in my pigeonhole; left that besom leaning on my car! Party faithful avoid me at dos in case I curse them.

CHIEF. Has made you a more effective Whip, though.

TIM. Damned straight.

DELIA (*looking at the screen again*). Ah. Miraculously the next amendment – amendment number five – has suddenly been called to vote. I wonder what reason Alastair might have right now for slowing the thing back down again. PM still in passport control, is he?

TIM. Don't let us keep you, Delia. I mean, grateful as we are that you chose us for your victory speech . . .

DELIA. This isn't my victory speech. That comes later.

She starts to walk out.

TIM. Bet your office smells of BO.

DELIA. It's a small price. I can open a window.

She exits.

TIM. Shit.

CHIEF. Yes. (*Breath.*)

TIM. No, but 'shit'.

CHIEF. I'm not disagreeing.

TIM. Fancy coming in to see us. Just to take her bow.

TIM *turns and falters. The* CHIEF *is staring straight at him.*

(*With a deep sigh of regret.*) You're doing that look.

CHIEF. 'Look'?

TIM. You have a look.

CHIEF. I've several.

TIM. This one's special: it's my turn to take a hit.

CHIEF. Alastair's dying on his arse there. Someone has to go down on to the floor right now and hold up the debate for us.

TIM. By getting out his willy.

CHIEF. Metaphorically.

Beat.

TIM. 'Someone'?

CHIEF. Mm.

TIM. Meaning me.

CHIEF. Meaning a soldier.

TIM. I'm a 'soldier' now?

CHIEF. Indeed.

TIM. Ten minutes ago I was half-weasel and half-worm.

CHIEF. Jesus Christ! Now's your chance to prove me wrong. Do you have to have your hissy fit right in the middle of a crisis?

Beat.

TIM. What do you want me to say?

CHIEF. A personal statement.

TIM (*very sceptical*). Really?

CHIEF. Urgent. Give it straight to Alastair.

The bell rings again.

TIM. Anything in particular?

CHIEF. You say the press has got hold of a story.

TIM. What story?

CHIEF. You find one! Embarrassing. Sordid. Ugly.

TIM. And my reward would be what? For committing professional suicide.

CHIEF. You sure you want to talk about 'rewards'?

TIM. I meant . . .

CHIEF. You think the VC is dished out in advance of the battle? It's an honour to lead us from the front . . .

TIM. So it's gratitude I'm feeling right now? I was having trouble placing it.

Beat. No one moves.

CHIEF (*quietly, trying to exclude* GUY). I can't pretend I was thrilled to have you join the team . . .

TIM (*quietly and conspiratorial too*). I have to say I'm shocked – you've done a really thorough job in trying to mask it.

CHIEF. . . . but maybe now you should think hard about your future.

TIM. Maybe you should save the rhetoric for someone who
gives a toot. Maybe I really am a self-serving little toad who
has no real interest in leading his side into battle.

CHIEF. Tim . . .

TIM. You're asking me to surrender my career out there! – Is
this how it usually works? Folks just smile and say 'No
problem'!

CHIEF. We're as good as our weakest link.

TIM. Well – look no further! Happy to accept the honour any
time you want to bestow it. (*He sits down purposefully.*) I
don't want to be selfish about this – if you'd like to lead the
troops and claim the glory – I'll just sit here and cheer you.

Pause. The CHIEF *buttons his jacket.*

CHIEF. Nineteen seventy-nine I first set foot here.

TIM. Oh?

CHIEF. They showered me with a thousand blue balloons in
my constituency . . .

TIM. I'd heard.

CHIEF. You think I won't abandon it in seconds – just to keep
my Party strong. You keep your eyes glued to that screen.

TIM. I certainly shall.

CHIEF (*marching to the door*). Loyalty is a rare bloom in
Whitehall – but in this office, Timothy, it blankets the
fucking walls and floor!

The CHIEF *strides up to the closed door. Beat. He raises
his hand to open it, and then his hand falls by his side.
Another beat.*

TIM (*coldly and impatiently*). Well?

CHIEF. Very hot. Very.

The CHIEF *teeters for a moment and then feints into his
chair muttering.*

GUY. Oh, my Christ! No. (*Yelling at Tim.*) Help me with him!

GUY *struggles to loosen the* CHIEF'*s tie.*

CHIEF. Unstable.

GUY. Yes. I saw.

CHIEF (*grabbing* GUY*'s wrist*). No! Not me, you goon. (*A rasping voice. Is he having a heart attack?*) This Government. (*Calling to Tim.*) You hear me, do you Timothy? 'Ten toes including the gouty one.' She's got us by the testicles.

GUY. Don't try to talk.

CHIEF. Don't nursemaid me, you tit. We just gambled everything and lost. (*This last declaration makes him cough. Gets his breath back. Looks at screen.*) Tim . . .

TIM (*drily*). Ah! Me again. Good-oh.

CHIEF. Tim . . . you must . . .

TIM. . . . I have to run round with my nob out. Super!

CHIEF. It's a long game. People forget these things. I'll see you all right.

He starts coughing.

TIM. Assuming you're not dead by half past nine tonight.

CHIEF. We've run out of options.

TIM. Well – time to claim our pensions. Fine by me.

CHIEF. We lose this and it's curtains in the morning. It's no longer just tent poles, Tim: it's the survival of our government.

TIM. No pressure then.

CHIEF (*to* GUY). You!

GUY. Me?

CHIEF. Can you sing?

GUY. What?

CHIEF. Can you? Sing him a World War Two song. Go on.

GUY. Actually, I'm thirty-six.

CHIEF. Everyone's grandmother sang them war songs. Think!

He points the cricket stump at GUY's *throat.*

GUY. 'Long way to Tipperary'?

CHIEF. Excellent. One two three go.

GUY (*starts to sing*). 'It's a long way to Tipperary, it's a long way to go . . . '

He continues under the dialogue.

CHIEF. Got you in the mood now?

TIM. Oh, definitely.

CHIEF. Right. I'll be in the next room dying if you need me.

The CHIEF *wobbles over to his office and opens the door. He leans on the doorframe.*

This is not the death of Nelson, mate. No one's gonna pop through that door and paint us. Arse in gear.

He goes into his office and slams the door. GUY *gradually stops singing, half expecting the* CHIEF *to rush back at any moment. He doesn't come. Eventually* GUY *falls silent.*

GUY. Poor bugger.

TIM (*to himself*). Poor nothing. Poor no one. Bloodhound hates my guts.

TIM *reaches for his Blackberry and starts writing a text. Next he dashes over to the safe and starts rooting through* Who's Who. *He is trying to see if it falls over at a particular page.*

GUY. What are you doing?

TIM. Someone's birthday.

GUY. What?

TIM. *Who's Who.* Someone's birthday.

GUY. You need to send a card?

TIM. It's the key to the safe, you drongo. If I can open the safe up we've got heaps of ammo. (*He gives up with the book.*) Bollocks.

He stares straight at GUY.

GUY. What?

TIM. Nibbles.

GUY. Now?

TIM. Remember nibbles, Guy? Remember what you said.

GUY. Well . . .

TIM. We had an arrangement, you and me. Your assignment.

GUY. What can I do?

TIM. You can go and save us.

GUY. Me?

TIM. I'll corral the votes . . .

GUY. Whilst I go to the slaughter. Don't think so.

He starts to leave.

TIM. We agreed, Guy. Cabinet by thirty-nine.

GUY. We didn't shake.

TIM. Nibbles!

GUY. I thought you meant planting a question. Not walking the fucking plank for you. No way am I going.

TIM. It doesn't have to be anything sleazy. (*Beat.*) What about just a point of order?

GUY. Can you think of one?

TIM. I've never read Erskine May.

GUY. Nor's anyone. If we make up a lot of old cobblers they'll only check it out.

Again, he is leaving.

TIM. Could obstruct the counting Whip, maybe. Make him turn away . . .

GUY (*sceptical*). When seventy votes are going past? You're going to need to cosh him.

He tries to leave again.

TIM (*jumping in his path, suddenly points at him with fire in his eyes*). They're going to out you as a homosexual.

GUY. Me?!

TIM. The press. Are going to out you.

GUY. Tomorrow.

TIM. And you deny it. You've just found out about the story.

GUY. And I've come in to *deny* it. Tricky.

TIM. Why? (*Breath.*) Oh, yes of course. We can't use that then. (*Beat.*) You're not into the rent scene are you . . . ?

GUY. Look . . .

TIM. I need to find something that we *can* deny. Spin out into a bloody long statement. Anything to buy us time. Only two amendments! (*Beat.*) You could always come out then.

GUY. I beg your pardon?

TIM. No time like the present. Tell the house you want to beat the press. I can get on the blower later and plant it in one of the papers for us. *Daily Mail* is tame.

GUY. In return for which you win the vote and my chances of reselection wither.

TIM. Oh, come on. Who cares? It's a compulsory phase, being gay. Like philately. Or Airfix.

GUY. I'm sorry, this is deeply personal. It doesn't affect my ability to open fêtes. It doesn't affect my ability to get farming subsidies. And I'm not going to sell it to the house just to buy you some time.

TIM. Not even for a PPS job. Four years from now. Junior Minister. Can be done.

The bell sounds.

Which Minister do you fancy?

GUY. I beg your pardon?

TIM. I mean which Ministry.

GUY. No.

Bell.

TIM. Three years.

GUY. Bollocks.

TIM. Come on, three. That'd be meteoric.

GUY. Meteoric rise to national laughing stock.

TIM. Two.

GUY. I'm not spending Christmas with the press sitting outside my door. 'Nibbles' is off, I'm afraid.

Long bell. GUY *tries to move.* TIM *gets in the way. It's becoming a child's game of tag.*

TIM. Come on . . .

GUY. Can you imagine it? I interrupt the tent poles bill to talk about my sex life. Imagine what the headline writers will do with the word 'camping'. It can only end in tears.

TIM. Two years!

GUY (*finally losing it*). This is the Conservative Party! Have you any idea how difficult it's been? Scouting for my first constituency – how many bridge rolls and cucumber batons I've eaten. Smiling at all the Tory ladies knowing the first thing they will always ask: 'When are we going to meet your wife, then?' It's cost me thousands to get my arsehole constituents to love me – mostly spent on raffle tickets! Umpteen tedious dinners with the Bishop; watching the Brownie's play rounders on wet Sundays. I even put on my fucking wellies and dragged supermarket trolleys from the river. Well now I've got them on side and I'm going to enjoy it for a while. I'm going to preside at my surgeries and wow them with my warmth and generosity. And when the time is right for Robin and I to do our shopping in Sainsbury's side by side, they will be so head-over-heels in love with me that none of them will give a tit about what we do with our evenings! Excuse me!

Now they are scuffling like little children.

TIM. We could let the protestors in. (*Freeze*.) Sally Gate in Whitehall they don't know about. Show 'em how to open it. Debate'll be suspended.

GUY. And I'll get hung by my balls from Victoria tower.

TIM. Only you and I know.

GUY. And the two hundred people in Kagoules on my tail. (*Beat*.) A year.

TIM. Waddya mean?

GUY. I'm not going to wait for two. A year until I get promotion. You want me to go down there now and help a gang of protestors invade – it's a year or nothing.

Beat. Offers his hand to shake. TIM *shakes his head.*

I don't give a tit if it's not honourable. You're shaking my hand right now or all bets are off.

TIM *shakes*.

TIM. We need them marching through the chamber. Speaker will adjourn.

GUY. And what will you do?

TIM. Grab our rebels by the balls.

GUY *exits.* TIM *sends another message on his Blackberry. Beat. A knock.* TIM *walks over to the lobby door and opens it.* MAGGIE *is there, clutching her folder.*

MAGGIE. Quite a thing out there.

TIM. MPs hiding in a toilet. Would make a meaty headline.

MAGGIE. You sent me a text.

TIM. I want your folder. (*Holds out his hand*.) There's rebels on the floor.

MAGGIE. And you need them.

TIM (*pointing to door where* GUY *has gone out*). I might have bought myself some time. I want to walk down there now and place that folder in his hands.

MAGGIE. And in return?

TIM (*nodding*). Mm. I'll give you what you want.

MAGGIE. A source.

TIM. Yes. A source.

MAGGIE. My piece will embarrass this office.

TIM. I'm aware. (*Breath.*)

MAGGIE. And suddenly you're willing to play? What happened to the famous unswerving loyalty?

TIM. You might ask.

MAGGIE. I'm sorry, I don't believe you.

Turns to go.

TIM. They're stiffing me.

MAGGIE. You what?

TIM. Unswerving loyalty. Doesn't exist. They tried to stiff me. Chief did.

MAGGIE (*sceptical*). Oh?

TIM. He's looking for a sacrificial lamb tonight. Wants me to go out on the floor and take a dive.

MAGGIE. And you're not willing to play.

TIM. I'm not willing to kibosh my career for the sake of a win.

MAGGIE. But you're willing to do it to him.

TIM. Tory values; survival of the fittest. Chief would kind of approve.

MAGGIE. You're a nasty little bastard.

TIM. So people have been telling me.

Pause. She wants to believe she's got him.

MAGGIE. The Deputy will know it was you. If it says 'A Whip confirmed' . . .

TIM. I agree.

MAGGIE. So . . .

TIM. I can give you better. I can give you number one
    bestseller. Your tiny folio is nothing compared to the truth.

MAGGIE. And you'd do that because . . . ?

TIM. Because tonight we'd win. You give me the file there: we
    win.

MAGGIE. The Chief gets stiffed. And you take a lap of
    honour.

    Emergency bell rings again.

    Needs to be pretty bloody dazzling.

TIM. Believe me. It is.

MAGGIE. I will believe you. Soon as you've said it.

    Beat.

TIM. I've got barely twenty minutes.

MAGGIE. I'm not giving you my only piece of ammo just for
    promises. I sat in here only two hours ago listening to your
    adjutant giving me his lecture: the loyalty; the unswerving
    devotion. I want juice.

TIM. It's not that simple.

MAGGIE. Fine. I'll just pop out and watch you lose. (*Holds up
    the folder.*) This is gold dust, Tim, and you know it. The
    hippo alone is going to stuff my boss back in his shell. So
    shall we dispense with promises and you just bloody tell me
    what you know? It's my name on a book jacket or a
    confidence motion by this time tomorrow.

    TIM *goes to the drinks counter, pours himself a scotch and
    takes a long swig.*

    My God, just look at you fellas. Like someone's trying to
    get you to murder your kin.

    TIM's *Blackberry buzzes. He gets it out.*

TIM. Hang on.

He sends a text. Beat.

MAGGIE. Tim? (*Beat.*) It really is like sawing off a limb, isn't it?

She starts to leave.

TIM (*very quietly*). Drugs.

She stops. Beat.

MAGGIE. In Westminster?

TIM. In a manner of speaking.

MAGGIE. Come on . . .

TIM. Party conference. Last three seasons. Habit's growing. Hotels. Conference balls.

MAGGIE. Sorry. That's just not specific enough.

TIM. Top of the cistern in the gents by the ballroom in the Grand. That specific enough for you?

Beat.

MAGGIE. Coke?

TIM. Well, obviously.

MAGGIE. Names, Tim. I need names.

TIM. The Whips all know about it.

MAGGIE. That's their job.

TIM. Whips know everyone. Buying. Selling. The Whips have the veto on it. They decide who gets to sell. Gives them control.

Beat.

MAGGIE. Wait a minute . . .

TIM. Whips are the guardians of secrets. Every single MP, Maggie – everyone on your card – you have to know his sexual peccadilloes; you have to know if he does it with choirboys or baboons.

MAGGIE. You're accusing senior Whips of being dealers!

TIM. The Whips have been procuring tarts for centuries.
What's the difference? We buy guys off with peerages if
ambition's their drug.

MAGGIE. You're saying you have dealers on your books, Tim.

TIM. I'm saying we let that fella lay his wares out on the loo.

So far MAGGIE *has been too stunned to write. Now she
picks up her pen.*

MAGGIE. Who knows?

TIM. Everyone is involved.

MAGGIE. Alastair?

TIM nods.

You're gonna have to speak his name. I'm not writing this,
Tim. Not without hearing it out loud. Does the Deputy
know about it?

Beat. She stares hard at him.

TIM. Yes.

MAGGIE. Say it.

TIM. Yes.

MAGGIE. Say it.

TIM. Yes.

MAGGIE. Say his name. Say it.

TIM. Alastair knows.

*Beat. A wide grin spreads across her face. The lobby door
bursts open.* ALASTAIR *is there. He rushes in and fails to
notice* MAGGIE *for a split second.*

ALASTAIR. Did you not hear the bell ring, Timothy?

*TIM and MAGGIE notice the chaos on the monitor for the
first time.*

(*Pointing at the monitor.*) Floor's been invaded by a chorus
singing 'Valderie'.

MAGGIE. Look at them!

ALASTAIR. Gives us half an hour to get to work . . . what's she doing here?

MAGGIE. Tim appealed to my sense of duty. (*She hands the hippo to* TIM, *but not the file.*) Be careful. Don't damage the inscription. Take that to Skywalker and tell him to call off the rebel force.

TIM *looks apologetically at* ALASTAIR, *then rushes out of the lobby door.*

ALASTAIR. Hold on . . .

But TIM *is gone.*

MAGGIE. All ended happily after all.

ALASTAIR. What did he give you?

MAGGIE. Nothing.

ALASTAIR. Look . . .

MAGGIE. You were right. Loyalty here – unassailable! Spent the afternoon trying to flog my poisonous wares. None of your boys would agree to play along. (*Breath.*) Thought I'd do the decent thing . . .

ALASTAIR. Whatever he said . . .

MAGGIE (*enjoying his discomfort*). You don't trust him? You surprise me. After all that arrogant crap.

ALASTAIR. Whatever he said . . .

MAGGIE. He said nothing. I thought I was going to be the one, you know – the Holy Grail – thought I was going to have you nailed. Sunday serialisation. Then the book. Then TV. Channel Four. Dispatches. All that juice in here and nowhere I can spill it. Just have to plod back to my photocopying.

She is about to leave.

ALASTAIR. Ellingworth.

She turns back.

MAGGIE. Well done

ALASTAIR. Your home. South Ellingworth. We have good researchers too. (*He reaches into his jacket and pulls out a single side of handwritten A4 – a letter of application.*) Didn't always have a burning ambition to be a journalist, did you?

MAGGIE. No. I didn't.

ALASTAIR. We turned you down.

MAGGIE. The Whips veto. Never saw my face or shook my hand. Just glanced at my CV, I guess. Turned down as unsuitable. Never even made it to the sandwiches. (*She advances a little into the room.*) I would have been good, you know. A good MP. A fighter. But I didn't attend the right schools.

ALASTAIR. It's not because of your background.

MAGGIE. No?

ALASTAIR. It's because you have no loyalty. We can tell.

Beat.

MAGGIE. Sure?

ALASTAIR. I'm sorry if it's galling for you – the press obviously relies on backbiting to ply its trade – but we in the Whips' office are simply incapable of acts of betrayal.

MAGGIE. Ah.

He smiles and she smiles back. She turns and faces the lobby door. Beat. She cannot resist turning back.

Would you care to comment on the story that the Whips permit dealers to supply cocaine to party faithful? (*Breath.*)

ALASTAIR. What?

MAGGIE. I was going to let you read it all on Sunday but your smug smile is really too much to bear. It's going in print and a Government Whip confirmed it. Though I shan't be naming him – I shall only be naming his superior.

ALASTAIR. He told you . . .

MAGGIE. Three hours. That's all it took – three hours to come in here and scale the Trojan walls. Tim is so bloody desperate to win tonight he tossed me your carcass in return for votes. So: you want to tuck your rhetoric away and make a swift decision on you future? I'm happy to leave your name out of it, but in return you'll have to give me someone higher.

Beat.

ALASTAIR. No.

MAGGIE. Chief's just one more cigar away from pulmonary embolism: would you rather end your career or his?

ALASTAIR. No.

MAGGIE. No one else is here. No one will find you. Whose name? Yours or Fulton's?

ALASTAIR. No. You don't understand how we function; don't understand what betrayal means . . .

MAGGIE. The hippo's just a taste. (*Waves the folder.*) You need to get this folder on the floor. You need to stick it in his lap if you want to have a government functioning.

ALASTAIR. This office . . .

MAGGIE. You think that your little boy's club is worth more than the party as a whole? (*Beat. No reaction from* ALASTAIR. *She changes tack.*) Twelve years in opposition. Twelve. Have you any idea how much people despise you?

ALASTAIR. We're back now.

MAGGIE. You put some rosy-cheeked heart-throb out front and scrape by neck and neck against a worn-out Labour party. That's not winning! Three votes is not a mandate to rule, you know. This party reeks of privilege and people will always despise it! Every time you mention 'Healthcare' or 'The welfare state' you sound like the Lady Bountiful throwing coins to urchins in the street. You're exclusive – you're elitist and superior and you wonder why the press can't resist you with your trousers round your knees? (*Beat. Gets closer to him.*) Imagine: your face and the word 'Cocaine' published side by side. It'll be the only thing about you people know. So – take a very deep breath for me and tell me who is 'Spartacus'? You or Fulton. (*Breath. Suddenly shouting at him.*) Tell me! (*No response.*) OK.

She turns to go.

ALASTAIR. Yes!

MAGGIE. Yes? What do you mean 'Yes'? 'Yes' to what? 'Yes' could mean anything.

ALASTAIR (*trembling, broken*). You know what I mean. Yes, he knew.

MAGGIE. Say the name. I need specifics.

ALASTAIR. Can't.

MAGGIE. Name of the hotel, then. Tim said it. Give me confirmation. Well? Confirmation.

ALASTAIR. The Grand.

MAGGIE (*a vicious leer*). Congratulations.

She waves the folder contemptuously under his nose and then drops it in his lap.

Didn't hurt anyone, did it? Fulton gets the rest he needs and you get his office, I would think. (*She gathers her things and goes to the lobby door.*) You can sigh with relief on Sunday that the Chief's getting barbecued not you. Human – like the rest of us.

She exits. Pause. ALASTAIR *visibly stiffens and opens up the file. He reads. After a moment the door opens and* TIM *creeps in.*

TIM. Ah.

ALASTAIR. Here he is, then. The Judas child.

TIM. Did she give it to you?

ALASTAIR. Better get it to his office right now. Since we've paid such a high bloody price for it.

TIM *takes it. Their hands pause on the folder together for a moment.*

TIM. What did you give her?

ALASTAIR. Silent anguish.

TIM. Yeah?

ALASTAIR. And what about you?

TIM. Eager. Corrupt. Disloyal. (*Beat.*) Confirmation?

ALASTAIR. Yes. (*Breath.*)

TIM. The Grand Hotel?

ALASTAIR. Uh-huh.

Beat.

TIM. Is there a Grand?

ALASTAIR. I imagine.

TIM. When are we going to tell her it's all cobblers?

ALASTAIR. Let her file the story first. Then I'll ring her editor.

TIM. Played.

TIM *is moving to the lobby door.*

ALASTAIR. Your play. Your text, Timothy. (*He holds up his Blackberry phone.*) Loyalty wins out.

TIM. And a healthy dose of bastardy.

TIM *exits. Beat. The door to the* CHIEF's *office swings open and he strides in with a mouthful of sandwich and an empty whisky tumbler. He is singing joyfully.*

CHIEF. 'It's a long way to Tipperary. It's a long way to go . . . '

ALASTAIR (*looking up at the monitor*). Letting the protestors in – bit extreme.

CHIEF. Maybe.

ALASTAIR. What did you do?

CHIEF. Heart attack.

ALASTAIR. Came through though, didn't he?

CHIEF. That's how they train the marines – by firing live
ammunition straight at their heads.

Scene Two

Music: 'The Christmas Song' by Ella Fitzgerald.

*Next day. 6.30 am. Upper Whip's office. A little sun struggles
to make it through the windowpanes.*

TIM *is asleep on an armchair wearing yesterday's crumpled
suit. He has a blanket over his legs.* DELIA *is swinging round
on* ALASTAIR*'s swivel chair as if trying it out for size.
Footsteps outside.* ALASTAIR *arrives for work looking neat
and elegant. He wears the same suit but a different tie. He
stops in his tracks as he sees* DELIA.

ALASTAIR. This is still my office.

DELIA. I knocked.

ALASTAIR. Then barged in anyway.

DELIA. Tim made a sort of a noise. Implied that I should
come in, I thought.

ALASTAIR. A sort of snoring noise.

DELIA. I may have misinterpreted. (*Beat.*) Does he often sleep
here, then?

ALASTAIR. Too far to get home; too near to claim a second
residence.

DELIA. Seventeen hotels? Eighteen? Isn't that was his dad
owns? He's hardly on the breadline.

ALASTAIR. Time there was we all used to sleep here – like a
gang of teenagers. Debates 'til three or four. Your damned
modernisation committee – you've taken all the fun out!

DELIA. Closed down the Boy's Brigade.

ALASTAIR. It was more than that, Delia. It was like a sort of trench camaraderie. You ask anyone who's been a Whip – their time in this office is the happiest that they've known. Pack hunting; the thrill of marching side by side; the only chance a politician gets to play for a team. That's why we willingly put up with the late nights and the early mornings. Spirit of the Alamo.

DELIA. Total cobblers. Chaps just wanted an excuse for staying out and drinking late. Avoid going home to their wives. This is parliament – it's not a private member's club. Mothers must go home and bath their children. Prime Ministers too. (*Breath.*) I can't see how democracy is served by running our committees on a diet of Pro Plus.

ALASTAIR. And yet here you are hard at work – six-thirty in the morning.

He wants his desk back – he goes over. She stands.

DELIA. Ah. You and I – we're the exceptions.

They are very close together.

Willing to spend Christmas alone; on call – just in case someone ends up pissed and in the gutter.

Closer to him now, intimate.

No one knows our sacrifice. Just you and I. Would be nice to share a turkey dinner . . .

ALASTAIR (*whispered, picking up on her intimate tone*). Why do I get the feeling that I'm being coaxed into letting down my guard?

DELIA (*very soft, very close*). Let 'em in through the Sally Gate, did you?

ALASTAIR. Yes, you're exactly the person I'd confide in.

DELIA. How did you nobble the ringleader? He even joined in the debate – expressed his full support. Must be something really sordid you had there.

ALASTAIR. And you came here just to congratulate me. Tell me that you understand.

DELIA. Who else would appreciate the artistry?

ALASTAIR. He just came to his senses.

DELIA. After forty-four ramblers broke up the proceedings. Gave you time to jump on the sucker. What d'you do?

ALASTAIR (*dry*). Gosh. For a second I almost told you.

He breaks away, sits at his desk and begins work.

DELIA. Five hours it took. Five hours spent debating the 'tent poles' bill. Only marginally less time than it took to debate kicking the living shit out of Iraq.

ALASTAIR. You're in a fanciful mood.

DELIA. I'm in a good mood. Let me enjoy it. I finally fucked you over.

ALASTAIR. You won by one vote, dear.

DELIA. Crucial one. (*Looks at her watch.*) Confidence motion in six and a half hours. What time did the PM get back?

ALASTAIR. Midnight.

DELIA. Bet he wishes he'd stayed on the golf course.

ALASTAIR. We have an honour system.

DELIA. Bollocks do we!

ALASTAIR. Existed since time immemorial.

DELIA. So has farting.

ALASTAIR. The Leader of the Opposition is honour bound to pair with the PM if he isn't here. Your leader swanned into the lobby with a Cheshire cat grin that made me want to vomit. It's a piss-poor way to win.

DELIA. I warned you all pairing was off. You thought I was being churlish. Six and half hours from now, Cinderella in his one slipper will be out of a job.

ALASTAIR. And that's what you came in to say.

DELIA. Actually I came in to think about colour schemes. Gonna have this whole place painted cream. White woodwork, obviously. Here we go again then. (*About to leave, then remembers.*) Oh. (*She produces a wrapped Christmas present from her bag.*) I bought you this.

ALASTAIR. How very generous! (*He opens it up. It is a new desk diary.*) Did you fill in the important dates for me?

DELIA. And leave you nothing to do?

She turns to go.

ALASTAIR (*calling after her*). Um . . .

He reaches into a drawer and produces and identical size and shape of present, all wrapped up.

Open it too, if you like.

DELIA. And spoil the enormous surprise on Christmas morning. (*She is leaving.*) There's a policeman on the Sally Gate so don't try it again.

ALASTAIR. Thanks for the warning.

DELIA. You're most welcome.

She exits. The sound of the slamming door wakes TIM.

TIM (*yawning*). Shit. We lost, didn't we? Wasn't a dream.

ALASTAIR. You worked hard last night, Tim-lad. Don't beat yourself up. Work to do.

TIM. What's the time?

ALASTAIR. Just gone six-thirty.

TIM. Better check my card. Confidence motion?

ALASTAIR. At half past twelve.

TIM. Phone round – ensure that everyone's on board.

ALASTAIR. Well, I wouldn't upset them by waking them all before dawn.

TIM gets to his feet. He isn't wearing his trousers – they are hanging on a chair. He finds a bottle of water. He uses it to drink, wash his face and smooth down his hair.

TIM. The duty Whip's breakfast. A scratch and piss and a good look round the office. Have you . . . ?

ALASTAIR. Phoned me at quarter past five this morning.

TIM. She did?

ALASTAIR. The editor. Would I repeat what I'd said about 'The Grand'? (*Breath.*)

TIM. And you told him . . . ?

ALASTAIR. I told him his reporter had been making up sources just to impress him.

TIM. Ouch.

ALASTAIR. They phone you?

TIM. Five minutes after. I mumbled the same and went back to bed. That's her sorted.

Beat.

ALASTAIR. She was a reject, you know. That's why she had it in for us.

TIM. Her hemline was too short for a Tory.

ALASTAIR*'s Blackberry buzzes. He answers.*

ALASTAIR. The Chief. Just arrived.

TIM (*acerbic*). His heart held out then.

ALASTAIR. Don't be churlish.

TIM. He scammed me.

ALASTAIR. He still knows how to make a play.

TIM. Why the hell couldn't he just ask?

ALASTAIR. Chief had his doubts but, take it from me, he doubts you no longer.

TIM. He really picks his moments.

ALASTAIR. There'll be another close vote. And another. And another. And another. Wouldn't spell the end if we'd lost last night – what matters is that we in this office are strong.

You came through, Tim. He asked you to prove yourself and lo and behold. It'll be cheese straws and toasts to you.

TIM *shrugs – he is content.*

Now then, let's knuckle down to today . . . Got to do some fancy footwork.

TIM. Six and a half hours. (*Breath.*) Maybe.

ALASTAIR *looks at* TIM. TIM*'s eyes are drifting towards the safe.*

ALASTAIR. Why do I get the feeling that we're going to have yet another discussion about . . .

TIM. Why not, though? Summon every charge on our cards, open the safe and wave his cock-ups under his nose.

ALASTAIR. And what then?

TIM (*patting the top of the safe*). Who's been shagging his chairman's teenage daughter – who's got into debt. We'll have them fondling our hems.

ALASTAIR. What happens in the horror films, Tim – when you finally set eyes on the monster? When it's just a lump of cardboard. The threat is gone. We can keep the threat as long as the safe stays closed.

The CHIEF *appears from his office wearing casuals – a jumper and sports jacket. He carries a handful of pens.*

CHIEF. All getting an early start today. Six and a half hours. Phone round. Take the temperature. Steady the nerves. I thought I saw a cardboard box here. (*Sees one.*) Yes! Could I just borrow it?

He empties some vote bundles out of the box.

TIM. You packing for the break?

The CHIEF *puts his cricket stump in the box – it is on the floor, abandoned after last night's 'heart attack'.*

CHIEF. Been hunting through my stationery drawer. Found a pen, engraved – it must be ten years old. 'Thanks for winning last night's crucial vote.' Haven't got a fucking clue who gave it to me or what vote he's meaning. 'S the odd thing about our job. We fight like dogs outside in the corridors. Pour all your energy into the charge – can't always remember what's written on the banner. (*He points to the sports trophy that contains pencils.*) Can you just pass me that trophy?

ALASTAIR *empties it, blows dust off and gives it to the* CHIEF.

TIM. You taking everything home for Christmas?

CHIEF. Not for Christmas, Tim. For good.

Pause. TIM *looks at* ALASTAIR *for an explanation.*

ALASTAIR. The intruders. Delia knows. The press will know pretty soon – she'll be on the phone right now.

CHIEF. Government Whips pull a stunt like that – let people in the lobby. Kagoules and whatnot. Curtains. (*Looks at the trophy.*) 'Backbencher of the year.' Marginals Christmas Dinner nineteen eighty-two. Made some speech: this that and the other. Made 'em laugh. Woke 'em up a bit. Little trophy to say 'Bravo'.

He exits.

TIM. He told me to suspend the debate.

ALASTAIR. He was testing you and you came through, yes. Bit extreme. But someone's head must roll.

TIM. And he's . . .

ALASTAIR. Finally you understand loyalty, Tim. You proved yours to him. The Chief knows how to reciprocate. Well now, breakfast beckons. See if I can steer him away from the buffet. He's really a bugger for his sausages and I'd like him to enjoy his retirement. (*Leaving. Turns back.*) PM's birthday.

TIM. What?

ALASTAIR. The code. Thought it was obvious, really. PM's birthday. (*Beat.*) Open it. Go on. Open it.

TIM. I thought you said . . .

ALASTAIR. The collected indiscretions of the last fifty years. You can be in charge of today's campaign – can set up a stall by Churchill's statue and hand out blackmail notes. I'm serious. One nine one oh sixty-six. The PM. It's Armageddon – so let's not get caught napping. Are we gentlemen or are we warriors? I trust you to make the right choice. Check your card.

He pats TIM *on the shoulder and exits.* TIM *pauses and then starts to dress. He is about to exit and then he glances at the safe. Pause. Contemplation. He walks over to it and considers it further. He has to know. He picks up the copy of* Who's Who *on top of it.*

TIM (*finding the entry*). Oh nine. Ten. Sixty-six.

He reaches to the safe and uses the numbers he has just found as a combination.

Oh nine. Ten. Sixty-six.

The safe door swings slowly open. We cannot see what is inside it. He stares. Pause.

Cunning.

Blackout.

Music: 'I Wish It Could Be Christmas Every Day' by Wizzard.

A Nick Hern Book

Whipping it Up first published in Great Britain as a paperback
original in 2006 by Nick Hern Books Limited, 14 Larden Road,
London W3 7ST

Whipping it Up copyright © 2006 Steve Thompson

Steve Thompson has asserted his right to be identified as
the author of this work

Cover image by Martin Rowson
Cover design by Ned Hoste, 2H

Typeset by Country Setting, Kingsdown, Kent CT14 8ES
Printed in Great Britain by Cox and Wyman, Reading, Berks

A CIP catalogue record for this book is available from
the British Library

ISBN-13   978 1 85459 957 7
ISBN-10   1 85459 957 5